PLAY WITH A SMILE...
Funny Stories in
Rugby League

Maurice Bamford

VERTICAL EDITIONS

First published in the United Kingdom in 2005 by Vertical
Editions, 7 Bell Busk, Skipton, North Yorkshire BD23 4DT

ISBN 1-904091-12-1

Cover design and typeset by HBA, York

Printed and bound by The Cromwell Press, Trowbridge

CONTENTS

ACKNOWLEDGEMENTS

I would first like to thank the wonderful players I've worked with over the years and other characters in the brilliant game of rugby league who have provided me with superb and often funny memories on which this book is based. I also want to thank John Boyd for writing the foreword and for the entertaining times we have shared on the radio.

Special thanks are also due to Robert Gate for letting me use the fabulous old photos in this book from his magnificent collection and to ruby league photographer, Sig Kasatkin, for providing the excellent pictures of Kevin Ward, Andy Farrell, Mike Gregory and Joe Lydon.

And last, but certainly not least, I would like to thank my dear wife Rita for the love and support she has given me in my career and throughout our lives together.

Maurice Bamford
March 2005

FOREWORD

I once read somewhere that you either have character or you are a character. There is of course a distinct difference between the two applications of the one word. So dwell on this for a moment – what if you really are both? I'll come back to that in a moment.

In the meantime if there is one man who I would always sit down and listen to when he starts to tell me a tale it's Maurice. He has that natural ability that is given to very few of us, that ability to make an audience, whether it be one person or one hundred, sit up and listen. The best bit is that his stories invariably have a funny ending. I've lost count of the number of occasions when I've had to hold my sides when hearing him give forth. I'm seriously tempted to relate a couple here and now but I wouldn't want to incur his wrath, not for a ransom!

There is just one little story that I feel justified in telling and it occurred when Maurice was the coach of Leeds. This mighty organisation had turned to local boy Bamford to relight the blue touch paper of their fortunes and he was on the case immediately. He would have walked barefoot from his origins in Kirkstall Road to answer the call and when it came, as with the summons to take charge of Great Britain, he was ready, it was his time and he was going to enjoy it to the full.

One of my tasks as local radio sports editor was to gather opinions from the great and good and I usually did it during waking and working hours. For some reason, and it escapes me now, Maurice said he would only be available in the evening and that I was to travel to Headingley where he would meet me. I arrived in good time on a dank autumnal evening; you know the kind – when you run your hand over any outside surface to discover it's damp and cold. Maurice was as good as his word, he met me in the car park and ushered me into the referee's room. A large notice on the wall read: *At this club we have a 15 minute interval at half-time.*

I was impressed, fancy telling the ref how long to take. Only a big club would dare.

Once sat comfortably I began by releasing the pause button on my recording machine, it was called a UHER after its manufacturer and it had a reputation for producing superb quality but was damned heavy to cart around. It was the old style reel-to-reel quarter inch tape.

Maurice was on great form and I was secretly rubbing my hands as he gave me some great stuff. After about ten minutes and whilst the coach was in full flow I took a peek under the lid, just to ensure the tape hadn't snagged and that's when the horror hit me – I hadn't got any tape in there and the two plastic reels were whizzing silently round and round!

It dawned on Maurice at about the same time as it hit me, we looked at each other, my mouth fell open and his roared open, with laughter I'm glad to say.

Being the kind of bloke he is, we had a break and did it all again and he was just as good the second time.

It's in that kind of atmosphere that friendships are forged, friendships that stand the test of time. And by the way, in case you hadn't spotted it already, Maurice is a big character who has enormous character, read on and enjoy.

John Boyd
Sports Presenter, BBC Radio Leeds
February 2005

INTRODUCTION

As the brand new era of Super League dawned in 1996, those of us already so long associated with this wonderful game and with a background stretching from the end of the Second World War (and in some cases even earlier), never realised how quickly rugby leagues traditions would be hidden in the mists of time and dazzled in the glitter of full-time players, and *Sky Sports* TV coverage.

Like many people of my era, I was brought up with the game in the City of Leeds which boasted three professional teams – Leeds, Hunslet and Bramley – and one of the toughest amateur leagues – the Leeds League – in the country.

In the days immediately after the 1939–45 world conflict, Leeds enjoyed the magnificent surroundings of the fabulous Headingley Stadium, where huge crowds of sports hungry fans would flock to watch their favourites in blue and amber (although I recall as a lad the jerseys being tangerine, with black shorts) without a trace of instant replay on the big screen.

The superb Hunslet played at the beloved Parkside ground with its all timber boardroom, dressing rooms and players' after-match eating area. Around the pitch perimeter was a picket fence with the teams emerging from the old cricket field side of the grandstand through a little wicket gate and onto the field. And like many of the grounds in those days, the bath at Parkside was a communal one and it was not unknown for on-field arguments to be continued in the bath after the game.

I am told that the original colours of the club were chocolate and white. Colours worn with pride, but my first glimpse of this wonderful club's strip was the famous myrtle, flame and white.

Bramley were one of the last clubs to play at their original ground with its 'interesting' dressing rooms until the early 1960s when the then new McLaren Field was built and played on. Before that, from day one, the club played on the field directly behind the Barley Mow pub in Town Street, a pub that still stands and is shrouded in rugby league history, as it was for many years the club's headquarters and boardroom. The dressing rooms, as anyone who remembers the old Barley Mow will recall, were in the loft of the pub with access through a door at the side of the building and an old open staircase leading to the loft with a rope handrail down one side. The timber treads were gnarled with the years of studs grinding and gouging grooves into them as players took the field and returned eighty minutes later, or earlier if caught misdemeaning by the referee. The bath at the Barley Mow was at the bottom of the dreaded open staircase and both teams had use of this Spartan, archaic cleansing aid after each match, but the outside door had to be left open to allow the steam to escape or all the players clothes would be sodden as the steam rose up into the dressing loft. Because of the door being ajar, this area was the haunt of many of the young ladies of Bramley, hoping, no doubt, to see more of their heroes than normal!

These were only three of the clubs which, with many more, produced a part-time professional game that enthralled millions of spectators over the years and laid a platform from which today's tremendous Super League emerged. Those early days saw teak-hard men involved in the game at six-inch centres. Hard, humorous men, several at every club, who worked in the coal mines, the steel works, in the foundries, in teaching and on the building sites, then trained for their sport in the evenings in snow, rain and frost. There are stories of men working the afternoon shift down the pit, and then running from work straight to training, doing their stuff and then running home for a bath. One tale of folk law is of the famous St Helens and Widnes international forward, Vince Karalius, who it is said regularly ran after training at St Helens to his home in Widnes. Another is of two famous Wigan players selected to play for Great Britain against New Zealand at Central Park, who arrived at the ground in 'their muck' for the international match after working the morning shift down the pit.

These were days too of big crowds and very little pre-match entertainment by scantily dressed cheerleaders or Bullman or Ronnie the Rhino. There may have been a brass band marching and playing (but only if the grass was dry) or the odd junior team curtain raiser in good weather, but mostly the crowds flocked to see the game – and how they flocked.

As a kid in 1947, I was at Headingley to see the Leeds versus Bradford Northern league game on the Wednesday evening, in amongst a crowd of over 43,000 to watch a drawn game after the Saturday Wembley Cup Final between the same two teams. In the early 1960s I was at a full house at Central Park, Wigan, to watch a mid-week cup tie replay in which Wigan won convincingly. And in the cup final replay of 1954 at Odsal between Warrington and Halifax, I was present along with over 102,000 others in a record crowd that witnessed the great 'Wire' side lift the old trophy. Yes, times change – as do peoples needs for entertainment – and today some of the statistics of those far off days seem incomprehensible.

Mr Harry Jepson, one of the great elder statesmen of our game and my chairman when I was coach at Leeds in 1983–84, tells of a game at Parkside when Hunslet played Leeds in front of a crowd of over 19,000. The after-match balance sheet shows, '£9.10 shillings paid for Police supervision, plus 5 shillings to be shared by the 10 constables on duty as a gratuity in place of expenses'. That is two and a half pence each in new money, absolutely true!

Another statistic from the same match was the amount of revenue collected from the old cinder car park, at the opposite side to Mother Benson's end, a total of £3, 5 shillings for 16 motor vehicles parked. This was for a gate of over 19,000 – the mind boggles. Youngsters of today may ask, 'How on earth did 19,000 people get there with only 16 vehicles?' Well in those days you walked or got there by tram or bus. But the real question for those who can remember the place is 'How on earth did they get 19,000 people into Parkside?'

This book though is not about statistics, it's about the humour and the pathos, the characters and the antics they got up to, the old stars who sported the broken noses and cauliflower ears as badges of honour, men who you hated for eighty minutes but could enthral you for hours in conversation. Like the late and very dear Graham 'Grabsy' Wilson who as a young man signed for the Hunslet club. Having just signed, he was not known to the gateman when he went to play his first game and the official would not let him in until Grabsy had paid his three shillings and six pence to get into the ground. He then saw one of the club's directors selling the match programmes and went up to him to complain about the entrance fee. 'So you had to pay to get in, did you? Well, you had better buy a programme to see if you are playing then,' said the director.

It's about our game, the North Country game and the

wonderful men it produced. Men who played in only three counties for many years – Yorkshire, Lancashire and Cumberland – even though the game was offered to the south and to Wales, it did not flourish until 1980 in London, and not until the advent of professionalism in the principality. It's about the men who regularly beat the Aussies and about a few men who were not internationals but were men I knew, and possibly you knew. Men who you may remember as players or coaches – not all household names but good men.

One man who played for the Leeds club, was an international player in his own right and a tourist on the first ever tour of Australia in 1910. On more than one occasion he had to be released from Armley gaol on bail to play for Leeds as he liked a drop too much and would be in the nick on a drunk and disorderly charge, but he was far too good a player to leave out of the team. That's the sort of days they lived in, with little periods off work for any leisure time, a few pints and their chosen sport. And if you were a professional player then that was a huge help with the family finances.

Sadly not all of them are still with us, but hopefully some of these tales will remind you of them and I hope you will enjoy this stroll down the lanes of yesterday amongst the great company of real men, the men of rugby league.

1

COACHES

BILL SMITH

Bill Smith was the quintessential Welsh stand-off half, quick thinking, tough, skilful and a good organiser. He was also the best coach I ever played for. I say played for because that's what Bill would have wanted, not to play under him, but for him. His gift was to make you feel special, the ability to improve your game through a quiet word, a short story about his career that dovetailed into the point he was making about you and he always left you with the answer. His man management was outstanding and almost everyone who worked with him would have run through a brick wall for him.

Bill came North to play for Batley from South Wales in the 1920s and was an immediate success with the then well respected small Yorkshire woollen industrial town's supporters. Injury curtailed his league playing career and he went into coaching at Morley Rugby Union Club, as did Bill's long-term mate, the legendary Ben Gronow, the Huddersfield and Great Britain goal-kicking forward. Bill made his name as a league coach when he attracted the attention of the great Leeds club and took the side to Wembley to win the Challenge Cup by 18 points to 2 against Warrington in 1936. He was back as a Wembley winner in 1953 when coaching Huddersfield to a 15–10 victory over St Helens in a game remembered as 'Peter Ramsden's' final when the teenager won the Lance Todd trophy on his birthday.

I came under Bill's influence when I was transferred from Hull to Dewsbury in 1956 and the great man was heading towards retirement in coaching and was assistant coach to one of his former players, the one and only Lionel Cooper the tremendous Australian Test wingman and another legend at the superb Huddersfield club. Bill's lilting rugby-steeped Welsh accent had an almost hypnotic effect on those he was addressing and his use of rugby jargon made him especially interesting as he spoke of taking a pass directly from the dummy-half as 'Take it up first cab off the rank' his need of the forwards to work hard in the game would be explained thus 'We need someone to carry the piano and someone to play the bloody thing, so the forwards will carry it and the backs will play it'. Bill's policy on defence was simplicity itself, he would explain that all a defending team had to do was take the first step – that was to stand opposite an opponent and don't miss the tackle. As for the sliding defence, Bill would suggest the 'paling fence mad dog technique.' Sounds complicated but in reality it was simple. The paling fence was our players in a line; the mad dog was the opposition carrying the football. While ever the palings were there the dog could not get through, but should one paling not be there the dog would get out and bite you!

Bill could turn on the humour too and his tales would help pass the time on those long bus journeys before the motorways were built. One tale involved the final Welsh trial at the old Arms Park. Bill was at fly half (stand-off) for the Possibles and at open side flanker for the Probables was a giant of a man, one Dr Llewellyn. Now Bill had crossed swords with the good doctor before and had never come out on top – as was the case with Llewellyn's first tackle on Bill which resulted in Bill's eyebrow requiring three stitches. But with a Welsh Cap at stake, a mere three stitches would not keep a good man out and Bill returned to the game determined to gain retribution. As Dr Llewellyn's head popped out of a ruck Bill saw his chance and a mighty swipe of his boot was going on target to the doctor's cauliflower ear – until one of Bill's own forwards stuck his boot in the way and Bill broke his little toe in the collision. On the field again went Bill this time hell bent on damaging the doctor once and for all. Again Llewellyn's head popped out of a maul and, summoning up all his strength, Bill let loose his Sunday best punch to the doctor's chin – but he saw it coming, ducked his head and Bill broke two fingers on it!

The irony was that Bill missed out on the Welsh cap and the final episode was that as Bill was being looked at in the dressing room after the match, Dr Llewellyn, a renowned orthopaedic surgeon, looked in around the door and said, 'Do you want me to set those fingers Smith?' And not to be beaten Bill replied, 'No thanks doctor, on yer bike.'

The doctor just smiled as he had been selected for Wales. Bill came north the following month.

Bill lived for many years in the Pennine Hills town of Elland, between Halifax and Huddersfield, and years after we had parted company and I had moved into coaching, whenever I was involved in a game in that area Bill would come along and we would have a pint together and talk rugby league. I always remembered playing for Bill in the Yorkshire Senior Cup competition of 1960–61 when our Dewsbury side won 't'owd tin pot'. We beat several good sides on the way and, no doubt, were distinctly second favourites in every round, Featherstone Rovers, Bradford Northern, Leeds and Batley, at Mount Pleasant, in the semi-final. Then we beat York in the final at the old Crown Flatts ground by 15 points to nil and Bill was overjoyed, he made us feel like internationals when he pronounced to all and sundry, 'This win gives me as much pleasure as both my previous Wembley victories,' then gave us his famous rendition of 'Guide me oh thou great Jehovah' whilst stood on the rubbing down table in the dressing room! How great to think that Bill thought of us in the same light as Jim Brough, Eric Harris, Dicky Ralph, Stan Brogden, Dave Valentine, Lionel Cooper, Peter Ramsden and Ted Slevin.

In his later days he returned to his beloved Fartown as masseur and general help to the coach at the time and he died aged around 80 in 1980.

A wonderful coach and human being, Bill Smith, no better man to start this look at the 'old timers'. Thanks Bill!

GEOFF FLETCHER

Geoff will be remembered mostly for the number of years that he, almost single handed, kept the old Huyton club going as player, coach, secretary and chairman. He should also be remembered as an excellent forward, with a high work rate on attack and defence and very good handling skills, playing for some of the better Lancashire clubs in his time, notably Wigan, Leigh and, I believe, a spell in Cumbria at Workington Town.

A St Helens lad, Geoff was a renowned character amongst many great characters in those days and referees gave him leeway to help his sometimes struggling Huyton team during games. Not that any referee allowed Geoff to cheat or break the rules of the game in any way, but leeway never the less. Let me explain.

While I was coaching Huddersfield in 1980 we went on Easter Sunday to play at Alt Park, Huyton. Geoff was watering the pitch when we arrived and I went for a cuppa with him up to his office. He told me that he had a lot of amateur players in against us and although he had coached them on Tuesday and Thursday evenings he was not sure if they had taken in all what he wanted them to do.

The game started and after about 10 minutes, with the score 15 points to nil to us, Geoff suddenly pulled out of a scrum, had a quick word with the referee and walked over to his three-quarters and proceeded to stand them in a better defensive position, then returned to the scrum, said thanks to the referee and the game proceeded. Just before half-time, Huyton worked a move from a tap penalty but it broke down because a forward ran into the wrong position and dropped the ball. Geoff again said to the official, 'I won't be a minute, ref' and physically set the move up again with the Huddersfield team and the referee stood watching. Then when he asked if they could just go through it once more, the referee said 'No Geoff, now come on!'

Now this truly happened and this is why Geoff Fletcher must be remembered, mostly because he wanted his players to be professional about their game, but more importantly, he kept the age-old rugby league image of likeable, experienced characters alive in the non-rugby area of Harold Wilson's constituency.

Geoff owned a very good pub in St Helens and had a manager run it for him whilst Geoff conducted business at his farm. It was a cracking Friday lunchtime pub and popular with the building trade workers of the town. Geoff was awakened early one Friday morning, around 5 o'clock, by a phone call from his manager. 'I won't be opening today, Geoff,' the manager said, 'I've just awakened to find my partner has passed away.' Geoff had to think quickly as there was no way he could afford to miss Fridays takings. 'Oh dear, I am sorry,' said Geoff. 'It must have been quite a shock to you, but if you take my advice you will open as normal. It will help to take your mind off it.'

In the heady days of a couple of back to back wins at Huyton,

Geoff made unusual plans to transport his team down to the capital to play London Crusaders, the fore-runners of today's London Broncos. Unusual because he would cut out the day long bus trip and fly the team south and get there in no time at all.

Now Geoff had a mate with connections in the aeroplane business who could get a good deal for Geoff and arrangements were made and a time agreed for the Huyton team to be at Manchester Airport on the Sunday morning of the game with a flight back straight after playing. Great, thought Geoff and all the team, excited about the new-fangled way to get to a match. On the day Geoff and the lads were ushered out onto the tarmac to board the plane. Looking around all Geoff could see was an old bi-plane with little round windows in the covered section and an open cockpit!

'Hello,' said this voice from behind Geoff and turning he saw a man dressed like Biggles with a leather flying jacket, fur lined boots and a leather helmet with goggles. 'Are we ready then?' asked Biggles, tossing Geoff another leather helmet, 'You'll want your overcoat on. It gets cold up there, and don't forget a scarf,' he said to Geoff.

By this time all the players were on board, filling the enclosed seats, laughing and giggling at the fun of it all, but Geoff had some questions to ask the pilot. 'Does this aircraft have radar and have you registered a flight plan?' asked Geoff.

'No to both old chap,' replied Biggles, 'we don't require either. You see we will be there in around two to three hours and London is south as the crow flies.'

Geoff was not amused, 'How do you check your bearings?' he asked.

'That's easy; I find the M6 then on to the M1 and follow it straight to the capital.'

'What if it's foggy and what about the flight home tonight in the dark?' asked a now worried Geoff.

'Oh, easy,' was Biggles reply, 'in the fog I just fly much lower, cut the engine and listen for the traffic and at night I just follow the lights, old boy, just follow the bally old lights.'

Needless to say the pilot was flying them down to the smoke on the cheap. Geoff was sat in the open cockpit on the trip down but made sure he had a covered seat on the homeward journey!

In Geoff's time the old Huyton club, which had been Wigan Highfield, Liverpool Stanley and Liverpool City, became Runcorn Highfield and later Prescot. But it was as the Runcorn Highfield club that Geoff once related a true tale to me. It came to pass that Geoff had signed a big, strong forward from amateur football in the St Helens area. The kid had the reputation of being a fighting man and one who would not take a backward step. On signing the kid in August, just before the season's start, Geoff handed the player £500 with a promise that, if all went well, there would be another £500 for him the week before Christmas.

The player kept his nose clean as his part of the bargain and the week before Christmas, after training on the Tuesday night, Geoff was on his way to a board meeting at the club ground when he bumped into the player who had not received his £500 and was upset to say the least

'Fletch, where is my money?' said the big forward. Geoff was a little irate that the kid should address him with such irreverence and replied, 'I said you will get your money and you will but you don't expect me to carry all that in my pocket do you?'

The player had lost his composure now and said, 'Listen, if I don't have the money by tomorrow, you will get that.' and thrust a ham like fist into Geoff's face.

Now, as most people knew, Geoff was a hard lad, a big fellow too and a former professional boxer as well as a respected front rower so he was no pushover, but he was much older than the player, old enough in fact to be the player's dad. 'Let's have it now then,' said Geoff and the two got at it there on the grass outside the boardroom. After about 30 seconds Geoff knew the player had too much for him to handle and worse still he was being messed up with mud from the field on his freshly cleaned overcoat. His shirt which his mum had washed and ironed was torn, his tie was dishevelled, his trousers full of mud and his wig well out of centre. Some other players came out and broke up this one-sided affair and Geoff staggered into the boardroom. Geoff's vice-chairman was already waiting for him and seeing his plight said, 'What on earth has happened to you Geoff?' Sipping a whisky, Geoff said, 'I've just been negotiating a contract.'

Not many chairmen have that trouble.

As I mentioned earlier, in his younger days Geoff was a very promising professional boxer, a heavyweight, and his trainer and manager was one of the famous Chisnall brothers of St Helens. When Cassius Clay, now Muhammad Ali, came over to Britain to fight Henry Cooper on the second occasion in 1966, one of his American sparring partners wanted a fight over here to make a few quid and this unknown heavyweight was matched with a young Geoff Fletcher in a four-rounder at Liverpool Stadium on a very good bill. Now Geoff was well fancied as he was unbeaten in eight bouts and, as Graham 'Swazzer' Swales found out years later when he nicked his wig at Huddersfield, Geoff could bang a bit!

No one remembers the boxer who faced Geoff that night but as Geoff says, 'I looked over to him when I entered the ring and I thought I was hallucinating. I had heard of big heavyweights but this bloke made me look like a welterweight and I was a big lad.'

Nevertheless Geoff answered the first bell and led with his good left jab – and that's when the lights went out. Bang, bang, bang, a left hook, right cross and another left hook knocked Geoff out of the Liverpool ring and almost out of the city. Geoff thought the Yank had hit him with the bell as all he could hear was a boom, boom, boom!

He landed on the writers' desk top which surrounded most of the ring and although he was conscious, each time he tried to rise to climb back in the ring he found that his balance had gone and he fell over again several times and was counted out in one of the shortest bouts in boxing history. Geoff couldn't understand why he kept falling down and was advised that this was a normal reaction to a heavy punch that fuddled your brain but he insisted that he was fully in control except for repeatedly losing his balance. Then Geoff realised what had gone wrong. As the referee was counting him out Geoff was rising from the writers' table and the table had a slant to allow the writers a better angle for their paper to rest on, so in his bemused state his feet were not coming down level, hence he fell at each step. He decided then to concentrate on his rugby and forget ever becoming heavyweight champion of the world! Geoff Fletcher – a legend.

LES PIERCE

Les was a big, strong second rower from the heartland of Wales. His partnership with Albert Fearnley formed a fearsome combination for Halifax when most clubs had two hard men in those positions. Like most tough forwards of his day, Les was great company and a very humorous man. And with his rugged good looks (he was a lookalike of the film actor, Robert Ryan) Les was the life and soul of any party.

But he had one weakness, he just could not remember names, well, not all names, but some would not stick with him, as one tale of when Les was coaching Halifax explains.

Halifax had signed that excellent wingman, Peter Goodchild, from Doncaster. Peter, a Yorkshire County class finisher on the wing, had fair hair but was becoming decidedly thin on top. Now at the time he was at Doncaster the South Yorkshire club also had a particularly good forward called George Goodyear, and he too had blonde hair and Les rated the big forward highly. Because of his failure with names, for almost two years at Halifax, Les called Peter, George.

This grated on Peter's nerves and culminated one night at training when Les called the Halifax first team to the bottom of the Thrum Hall pitch to prepare for the weekend game. Peter was playing touch and pass with the A team lads and did not hear Les call. Noticing Peter was missing from the squad, he called up to Peter, 'George, come down by here.' Peter heard him this time and thought, no, not until he calls me Peter.

Les called again, 'George, come down by here.' With still no movement from Peter, Les called over Terry Dewhirst, his prop forward and said, 'Terry, go tell that bald headed bugger from Doncaster that I want him' and that was after two years!

Les was the type of coach that players love. Tough, uncompromising, no nonsense, straight John Bull and he coached at many clubs, including taking the Welsh World Championship team to Australia and beating England there in 1975. He coached Leigh to a Floodlit Trophy Final win and did well at Bramley, building up a nice squad of players and making them a hard team to beat.

It was in one game for Bramley, in a cup tie at Salford,

where Les's warriors took on the might of a crack Red Devils team, crammed with internationals. After a mighty tussle the scores at full time were level, resulting in a replay at McLaren Field on Wednesday the following week.

Now at that time there were two brothers who organised the touchline stand at the Willows. Both were huge, tough men and they were upset at Les's enthusiastic coaching from the bench, which was in front of their stand. As Les and his small band of staff walked back to the dressing rooms in great humour at the draw, they had to endure the banter from the stand, particularly from the two brothers who let their emotions run away with them and they verbally abused Les as he passed by. Les stopped dead, looked up into the massed faces of the crowd and called 'Which brave man said that about me?' The biggest brother called back, 'I did and hang on and I'll come down and say it to your face.' and with that he set off down the terrace, and Les waited for him.

As the giant brother cocked his leg over the stand wall to get onto the pitch, Les walloped him with a big right-hander and knocked him cold. Brother number two jumped over the wall but was dispatched before his feet touched the turf.

So Les had a double up and a treble if you count the drawn game because Bramley won the replay too.

Les had his bit of luck too in coaching, but don't we all. At Leigh, the Floodlit Trophy final was Les's first match at the club and imagine, Les, with his lack of names, being asked to coach in a final! He didn't know any of the team from Adam and with only minutes to play and Leigh behind by two points, he turned to his substitute and said, 'What's your name?' The player answered, 'Joe.'

'Right Joe, on you go onto the wing.'

Joe looked shocked, 'But I'm a hooker.'

To which Les replied 'Never mind that, get onto the

wing.' Joe did and in the last play of the game, Joe, who hadn't touched the ball until then, picked up a dropped pass, only inches from the line, and dived triumphantly over for the winner. Leigh had won the Trophy and the headlines in the following morning's nationals read, 'Brilliant substitution by coach Pierce wins cup for Leigh.'

Les was hard nosed enough to read through excuses too as the tale of the team meeting at Halifax shows. The then Thrum Hall side had a bad start to this particular season and Les called a meeting to thrash out the problems. As at most meetings to sort out faults, no one was to blame and Les waited patiently to write down the reasons for the poor performances as each player was asked for his version. Cracking scrum-half, Gordon Baker, was first to speak, 'I don't think we are training hard enough'.

International forward, Terry Fogerty, in typical forward mode said, 'Oh I don't think so Gordon. I think we are trained too hard'.

And so it went on, a valid point, then an excuse, all par for the course, as one would expect. Then, with Les's patience running out, Welshman Terry Michael, a fellow countryman of Les, held up his hand for a word, Les brought him in and Terry said 'I blame the physio, Les. For weeks now I've been telling him about my bad ankle and he says there is nothing wrong with it. I even asked him if there was a chance of having a plastic joint put in, but he said no.'

Les realised he was getting nowhere fast so he said, 'OK everybody out on the training pitch, but listen, Terry Michael, it's not a physio you need boyo, it's a bloody plumber!'

Like most characters Les attracted quite a few tales that were not exactly spot on in truth. But they are told with great respect for the man and in no way have I ever heard a tale that ridiculed the grand old forward. One I've heard told in Yorkshire, Lancashire and Cumbria was about a time when it was snowing hard, as it used to in Halifax, and Les had been upset at the lack of evasive qualities in his team as no-one was side-stepping or swerving. So Les told his team to wait in the dressing rooms until he called them and he disappeared out into the blizzard.

After about 10 minutes he came into the dressing room covered in snow. 'Right, everyone out,' he called, 'and stand in a line under the cover of the back of the stand.' Les faced the line of his players and shouted through the ever deepening snow, 'When I say go, start side stepping,' and suddenly uncovered hundreds of snowballs that he had made earlier and began hurling them at the players who had to evade the missiles by side stepping them. Some man, Les Pierce.

MAURICE BAMFORD

Please forgive my apparent lapse into egotism, but I too can recall things about my early coaching experiences that I think should be recorded. Like the time I started to distrust all team mascots, you know, the people who dress up in Tiger suits, or Rhino or Bull outfits.

I was at Bramley, in my middle spell and the side were playing very well indeed. The pack was big, tough and mobile and was composed of Tony Garforth, Peter Clarke, George Ballentyne, Karl Harrison, Alan Clarkson and the great Ken Loxton. It was the final game of the season and we were playing the Cardiff Blue Dragons at Ninian Park. The game was memorable to me for four reasons. Ken Loxton's back injury that forced his retirement as a player, Peter Clarke's retirement through old age, a terrific win by my lads and a run in with a bloody Blue Dragon!

Now this Dragon was mooching around in the dressing room area before the game, in fact it was there when we arrived on the team bus. It was about six feet tall, a perfect Dragon with scales, wings, forked tail and a long snout through which it breathed smoke. I had to ask this bloody Dragon to move its tail from the doorway when we arrived as the players could easily have tripped over it and injured themselves.

So we started the game against a decent Cardiff side that included Tommy David, Gordon Pritchard, an old player of mine from both Bramley and Huddersfield, plus several other good players, making them a hard team to beat.

Come half-time though and we were drawing when we should have had it won, consequently I was not in the best of moods as we approached the dressing room, and what was stood in the doorway, not allowing my players entry, but that bloody Dragon.

'Excuse us' I said as politely as possible but the Dragon shook its head, blowing smoke through its nostrils. Getting the hump by the second, I said more strongly, 'Move and let us in please,' again the Dragon shook its head and the smoke machine billowed further puffs of the smelly stuff in my face.

By this time all our players were queuing up, calling out 'What's the hold up,' and 'Come on, I need the toilet'. So in my sternest voice I said, 'Look, I'm telling you to bloody move yourself, for the last time.' and the Dragon puffed and shook its head.

Bang, I punched through the perfectly formed papier-mâché snout and the Dragon flew backwards at a rate of knots to land on its backside about five yards away with smoke billowing from every orifice. Slowly the Dragon removed the crumpled head to reveal a very shook up young lady. I was gob smacked, but a quick check that the fledgling Dragon was OK, and a swift kiss on the cheek and I was inside the dressing room to deliver a pep talk and eventually we won the game comfortably.

How was I to know that it was a lady Dragon, one Dragon looks very much like any other. Needless to say on the bus home I was 'Bamford, the Dragon Slayer.'

FRANK FOSTER

I could have told stories about big Frank as a rip-roaring second row forward. Tough as teak, a fearless pack leader and well respected throughout the game. In a time of characters at six-inch centres he was a leading candidate but it's from when he was a coach that this story about him originates.

The fearsome Cumbrian had moved clubs from Workington Town to Hull Kingston Rovers, and he had moved just about as far as the geography would allow in those days. He moved several more times, each time getting nearer and nearer to his native county: Bradford Northern, Oldham and finally, Barrow, just down the coast from Whitehaven and Workington.

The tale goes that Frank had been at Craven Park long enough and the Barrow board of directors wanted him out but the chairman, that grand servant of the game, Bill Oxley, wanted him to stay. Under pressure from his board, Bill thought of a scheme to get his way and he asked the secretary to type a letter to Frank, but not date it or sign it, stating that the club thanked him for his services but it was time to go.

Bill then asked for a volunteer to sign the letter and give it to big Frank that evening. No takers! No one wanted a face off with rough, tough Frank so each board meeting started with the same question, week in, week out, who will give the letter to Frank? No one ever responded to Bill's plea and it looked as though the crafty chairman had won his battle –

until a new board member arrived. He was a young solicitor who had just moved into the area and had a few quid to put into the club but did not know Frank or of his reputation.

At the next board meeting the dreaded question was asked and the new member astounded everyone by agreeing to hand the letter to the coach that night. The notice of dismissal was dated and the young solicitor signed it, sealed the envelope and went down to the pitch where Frank was conducting an unopposed session. As the new director approached Frank, the backs dropped the football from a set piece at the scrum. Frank went ballistic with the backs using language that blistered the paint off the Craven Park crush barriers. Eyes popping and red in the face with anger at the clumsiness of the backs, Frank turned quickly to confront the sacrificial lamb carrying the letter and never having seen the young man before yelled, 'And what the f****** hell do you want?'

Our victim realised his delicate position immediately and turning the envelope over pulled out his pen, and said 'Could you give me your team for Sunday, please?'

Frank did leave Barrow but it was when he wanted.

ROY LESTER
A good, big forward with plenty of heart and a dry sense of humour was Roy. We spent a couple of weeks together in Australia when he was coaching the old London side, Fulham. He was looking for a couple of Aussie players to bulk up his squad but the club was so short of money that Roy was skint, and seeing that I had a spare bed in my room, he stayed with me.

'I've got to save the money I have to make a good offer to the players I want,' explained Roy, when we were talking football one night, before going to sleep, I in my bed and he in his in the far corner. It had been a long day and I was half dozing, half listening to Roy talking about the players he would like when I heard him say, 'I have a meeting tomorrow with Steve Rogers and I think we may well be able to get him.' I suddenly realised what he had said and I sat bolt upright in bed, wide awake now, as Steve Rogers, was the all time great Aussie centre and was one of the famous 'Invincibles' who murdered us in 1982.

'Steve Rogers,' I repeated, 'how much is that going to cost, are you sure that you have enough cash to get him?'

'Oh yes,' Roy said 'I have about £200. Goodnight Maurice.' and as he turned around to go to sleep, he said 'Got you that time.'

It would have cost Roy £200 to speak to Steve Rogers in those days. Would a club today send a coach out to attract players without money? I think not.

2

FULL-BACKS

RAY DUTTON

Ray Dutton was a superb last line of defence and a great goal kicker. A big lad for a full-back, Ray introduced himself well in the tackle and, with his experience playing behind the ultra successful Widnes side of the 1970s and 80s he was a full international player and indeed a member of the very successful 1970 Lions tour. But this tale about the excellent full-back comes from his days at the back end of his illustrious career, when he had moved to the North West to play for Whitehaven.

I was in charge at Huddersfield in the 1980–81 season and had talked back into the game one of the finest ball winning hookers I ever saw in the days of competitive scrimmaging, Peter Clarke, of whom more will be said later. Now Clarkey was one of the old school, tough, with tremendous know-how in the scrum and years of experience learned the hard way.

I think there may well have been a touch of bad blood somewhere down the line between Ray and Clarkey because early in the game Ray Dutton just missed with a haymaker to Clarkey's chin, which brought a smile to Peter's lips and a quiet word to Ray in passing.

Now this game up in Whitehaven was being played the week before Christmas; the weather was cold and soon after the start of the game it turned to heavy snow. Late in the game, and with Whitehaven winning by around 10 points, Ray was tackled and fell in front of Peter, but the big full-back did not rise to his feet to play the ball, he just lay there in the snow. Peter must have accidentally caught him with his boot and Ray had an horrendous cut on top of his head. Off he went to hospital, the game ended, the players showered, went for a sandwich and a pint and the snow became a blizzard.

We were all in the old clubhouse bar when the door opened. The snow was blowing horizontally across the opening and in came Ray, supported by the physio. The players in the bar parted like the Red Sea to allow Ray to be led to the counter for some food and who should be stood, pint in hand in the front row but Clarkey. Ray Dutton stopped in front of Peter and growled 'You dirty bugger Clarkey,' and Peter, looking closely at the shaven head of Ray, with the blue stitches like a zip in his head and with fresh snow glistening amongst the cat-gut said, in an angelic voice, 'Oh dear Ray, how many stitches?'

Ray softened a bit and in a civilized manner answered, 'Seven.'

Peter took a swift intake of breath, 'Bloody hell Ray, it must have been a bad 'un, they only put five in a bag of taties.'

That's what it was like, no sympathy what so ever. No one messed with Peter Clarke, not even the good ones and Ray Dutton was a good 'un.

JOHN HOLMES

John holds the all-time record of first team appearances for Leeds RLFC. He played in every position for the club, except in the front row, and earned two benefits, equal to twenty years at Headingley, in a magic career that included caps for Yorkshire, England and Great Britain added to which he was a touring Lion.

A footballer par excellence, a goal kicker too, having

landed 100 goals in a season more than once and a player that other players rated. Better known for his exploits at stand-off half, John did play a lot at full-back and this tale comes from a game in which he was switched to the number one position for tactical reasons. The venue, Headingley, the opponents the 1982 Australian Invincibles.

With the visitors miles in front and with only a few minutes to play, Leeds were forced to drop kick out from under their own posts after one of a continuous stream of strong Aussie attacks. David Ward, the redoubtable Leeds captain, threw the ball to John to kick out.

'Where do you suggest I kick it, David?' asked John.

Wardy replied, 'Give it to him with the long hair, they won't come all that way back before it's full time.' pointing down field to Aussie test winger, Eric Grothe.

John did just that and Grothe skittled five Leeds tacklers in a 70 metre run to score. As the Leeds players gathered together under the posts awaiting the conversion and, hopefully the final whistle, John pulled Wardy to one side and said, 'Keep your bloody advice to yourself in future, David.' Great kid John Holmes.

ANONYMOUS.

One must always avoid hurting the feelings, even in light-hearted books such as this, of players who one has had a player and/or coach relationship. Some tales can be related using names but others would be too cruel to name the lad involved. Only he and I know the reasons for this next story and I feel certain that enough water has passed under the bridge so that the kid may have a smile in remembering.

It was at a West Riding club that I came across this young full-back whom I had inherited on taking the coaching job. Now this kid was a nice lad but his weakness was that he thought he was God's gift to the club and he should be playing for Great Britain, let alone in the A team of a then second division side. Falling a bit soft for the kid, I did my best to improve his play, after all, that's what they were paying (he laughingly said) me for and I kept him out along with the other full-backs on the books, working on drills and individual skills that would help them in game situations.

This young full-back was married and between his wife and his doting dad telling him he was miles better than he actually was, they were progressively driving a wedge between us which led to the player turning Bolshie against everyone at the club. My A team coach told me that he was becoming an embarrassment in training and was questioning the game plan and various moves my coaching staff and I worked out, so much so that the player was omitted from the A team for disciplinary reasons.

He just would not conform to getting down to regaining his place in my assistant's second team and yet demanded to be considered for a first team place. Now my first team were going through a successful spell and I told him he wasn't going to be considered in no uncertain terms. Then his dad phoned me, as did his wife, demanding his promotion into the top team and things got so bad that I suggested to his dad that he take him somewhere else to try his luck with another club, but no, this town was his birthplace and he should be in the first team, end of story.

This case was getting me down and it came to a head one training night when the kid button-holed me. He was quite an articulate lad, well educated and it did not seem right to rant and rave at him and use foul, abusive language but my kindness, after weeks of trying, was beginning to evaporate, quickly.

'You're no good as a coach.' he said, and I could see that he meant it. 'You have no time for me.' Now that hurt because I had gone out of my way to help the kid.

'Hold it, now that's enough.' I said in my sternest

headmaster's voice, but to no avail.

'Tell me, why am I always in the second team?' he said, leading with his chin.

'Because we haven't got a third team,' I answered. And that was the last time I saw him. I later learned that he joined the army and worked his way up through officers' college to become an officer. So he had something, but it was not as a full-back. I've often wondered if he ever realised the favour I did him by being cruel? I also wondered if he made the Army team, I very much doubt it, although as an officer he may have had a place on the selection committee.

Coaching is not all cakes and ale. Do they have the same problem in Super League, hmm?

BOB HIRST

I signed Bob at Huddersfield and he was a big kicker of the ball indeed and on ability earned his place in my Fartown team of 1980–81 at full-back. Bob, like several of the players at Fartown, had a weakness in that he was naturally thin. Light, but wiry, I think is the term.

Weight training and all the carb and protein diets in the world failed to build him up and he maintained his thin physique to the end. We had 'Thin' Terry and 'Thin' Mick at Fartown as well, indeed I once, as a bit of fun, selected a 'Thin' team to represent the club and had enough thin players to do so including reserves! We had 'Chubby' ones too but the main thing about those days was the great crack we had amongst the lads. Fartown was a happy club at that time.

JIMMY BIRTS

I signed Jimmy twice, for Halifax and for Wigan. At the old Thrum Hall he was magic for me, time and again winning games by scoring tries, kicking magnificent goals and making wonder last-ditch tackles, but at Wigan the surroundings and the club became too much for the red-haired lad to cope with and Jimmy was transferred to Carlisle and went out of the game still a young man and with plenty left in the tank.

In our promotion season at Halifax in 1979–80 we had to travel to the old Recreation Ground at Rochdale to play the Hornets in a crucial game and had to get at least a point from the game to maintain our challenge in the top two of the old second division.

In a humdinger of a game, with a bit of everything in it – including several all-in fights – we were leading 2 points to nil when the Hornets crashed over our line and kicked the goal to make it 5–2. And so it remained until the final seconds when our cracking scrum-half, Terry Langton, darted over behind the posts in the final minute. Then as the fiery half-back was coming back from scoring the try, he was flattened by a Hornets player and all hell broke loose again, fighting in lumps, as the Halifax boys took retribution for the foul on Langton.

In the ensuing melee Jimmy Birts was knocked out cold and was unable to attempt the simple conversion that would have brought us the two precious points. The reserve kicker, Dave Cholmondely, took the kick but he too had taken a bang in the fight and unfortunately missed the goal so the result was a 5–all draw, but it was enough to keep us in the promotion frame.

Jimmy went on later in the season to play a huge part in the team's tremendous Challenge Cup run and indeed, in the memorable 7 points to 3 victory in the quarter-final against first division Wakefield Trinity at Thrum Hall, saved our side with a tackle on ex-Rugby Union international, Mike Lampkowski, that ranks as the best man on man stop I have ever seen. Terrific tackle, close to our try line and Jimmy took man, ball and the touch-judge down in one go! Another great kid, Jimmy Birts.

3

WINGMEN

MICK SULLIVAN

There have been a number of great rugby league players called Sullivan. There was the fabulous Jim, the goal-kicking full-back of Wigan and Great Britain fame who captained the 1932 tour 'down under'. Then there was another captain of Great Britain, Clive, the Wales, Hull FC and Hull Kingston Rovers wingman who lifted the World Cup for us in 1972, and Clive's son, Anthony, another wingman who started at Hull KR but found fame as a try scoring sensation for St Helens.

But with all due respect, there was only one Mick Sullivan. His partnership with the great Billy Boston is folklore in the greatest game and the term 'Boston and Sully' slips off the tongue like milk and honey or Matthews and Finney!

The stories about Mick are legend, how he bandaged his right arm, from wrist to elbow, in the dressing room in Sydney before a Test match, then, after inspection by the officials, rubbed wet plaster-of-Paris into the bandage and 20 minutes later, the arm was right for some bone crunching tackles, mostly up around the nose area! Or when the touring Australians played the St Helens side the week before a vital Test match against Great Britain and because Mick was not playing in the club match, having been saved for the Test, his arch enemy and regular Aussie sparring partner, the teak-tough Peter Diamond, had knocked Mick's deputy wingman about. Mick reputedly collared him in the players' bar after the game and asked Diamond to try it on him, now if he wanted, but the big Aussie winger said he would wait until next week. He did wait and Mick gave it to him in the Test instead!

But Mick Sullivan has a theory about the why the Aussie tourists of 1982 and 1986 were so good. 'I know why the Aussies went unbeaten,' said Mick, 'You see I was on the 1962 tour and we fathered all these unbeatables between us while we were over there, that's why they are so good.'

You know Mick may just have a point there!

STAN McCORMICK

Stan was one of those excellent players your Dad told you about. A breed of player who could make the crowd in the best seats stand up whenever he received the ball. A side-stepper of the old school who could step both ways, inside and out!

The side-step was the classical wingman's trade-mark. Albert Johnson of Warrington had a fantastic step, so too the minute Australian, Len Kenny, who just after the Second World War, came over to join Leeds then crossed the hill to Leigh. Len could step all right but the middle back who set the ground at Headingley alight with his superb side step was the local Leeds lad, Johnny Feather, who died so tragically when returning home from a match in Lancashire.

Stan McCormick came out of the forces after the 1939–45 conflict and played for that grand old club, many years gone now, Belle Vue Rangers, and it was at Belle Vue that his try-scoring achievements came to the notice of St Helens. Now the Belle Vue complex in Manchester was known worldwide and amongst the many attractions were a circus, zoo, huge fun fair, National League speedway, wrestling, and of course, professional rugby league. A real magic haven in the dark, austere days of the late 1940s, the whole complex was managed by one general manager whose main job was to balance the books at the year end, show a profit and enjoy life!

Stan, his wife and young family lived in Oldham, which was only a short bus ride from Belle Vue. One Tuesday evening Stan arrived at the ground for training when a message came down from the manager that he wanted to see Stan in the office, urgently. Stan went up immediately and the manager asked Stan to sit down and passed pleasantries with him before saying, 'Now Stan lad, let's get down to business. St Helens have made a substantial bid for your transfer to them. Now I don't want to railroad you into a hurried decision, but you would help us out financially and do yourself a bit of good too if you joined them.'

Stan thought for a moment and replied, 'If it's all right by you I think I'll stay at the Rangers.' The manager's face changed colour several times as he digested Stan's answer. Stan continued, 'You see it's all about our young 'uns. When we play at Belle Vue, my wife brings the kids down to Manchester while we are playing, takes them around the zoo or fun fair or pops into the circus for an hour or so. I get my bath after the game and we meet up, get a bite to eat, and then go to the pictures in Manchester. Now if I go to St Helens, all that will change and I don't know if our lass will want to change it at all, so, no thanks, I'll stay here.'

The manager could see thousands of pounds drifting away from him on a whim of Stan's and the time had come for some straight talking. 'Now listen, Stan,' the manager explained, 'I've got to balance the books here at Belle Vue and I'm left with two choices. I can sell you to St Helens or sell Leo, the zoo's lion, to another zoo, but Leo is getting more people into the complex to watch him on a Saturday afternoon than to watch you, so Stanley, you've got to go.'

Stan saw the logic and moved across Lancashire to the Saints and enjoyed a good career there both as a player and twice as the club's coach.

Stan McCormick, a great and humorous chap and a wonderfully entertaining international wingman.

BARRY PARKER

BP as he is known to his mates was not an international wingman, nor a county wingman. He was one of those very good, strong running local lads that all who new him could not understand why he was not an international player. BP had everything in his armoury, tough, strong, fearless, deceptively quick for a well-built player, a hard defender who could knock forwards over as easily as backs. Like me, he hailed from the city side of the railway viaduct that to this day cuts across Kirkstall Road in Leeds.

As a junior pupil at St Simon's C of E school, he was invited to attend training for the Under 10s Leeds City Boys team and turned up to play in those kids' Wellington boots with the little rubber spurs on the heels. When asked by the teacher in charge of team training, 'Why are you wearing those Wellingtons, Parker?' BP, at nine years old replied, 'I all'us wear these to play in when it's wet!'

Some time after leaving school BP burst onto the scene in the very competitive Leeds and District league playing for the Leeds Electric side who were stationed and played at the Kirkstall Power Station grounds across the old ha'penny bridge over the River Aire, off Kirkstall Road.

The 'Lights' as they were known for obvious reasons, had a good side full of local lads. Then when the ultra successful team, the Milford, were formed, Leeds Electric amalgamated with the Milford and BP played there for a spell.

Later his professional career was rich and varied and his club CV excellent: Leeds, Wakefield Trinity, Keighley and Bramley, and BP scored many long-range spectacular tries for all his employers. But it was his antics off the field that endeared him to so many people around the Kirkstall area of the city. Always the 'Towny', BP's use of the English language was colourful to say the least but then he was a colourful character too and stories about his forays into the 'hunting, shooting and coursing' way of life are the subject of hours of humorous debate over a pint in the Cardigan Arms or the Milford Amateur RL club.

His business ventures are legend too and at some time or other BP has held directorships in the Burley Builders Co, Burley Debt Collectors Co and the Burley Security Co.

One hilarious story is of BP and his best mate who somehow gained knowledge of a price put in by a reputable painter and decorator to paint the outside of a very well-to-do house in far Headingley. Offering a price much lower than the proper decorator, BP and his buddy finished the job except for an area under the canopy over the front door. They had decided to spend a few days up at Appleby for the horse fair and had kept the money for the paint job with the owner of the house for safe keeping.

Wanting an early start to go to Appleby, BP and his mate set off, with the paint needed to finish the job, at about 3:30am and it was around 4:00am when they arrived at the house.

'Where are the step ladders?' BP asked his partner.

'I dunno' was the reply, so at 4:00am BP balanced his mate on his shoulders and manoeuvred the acrobatic painter under the canopy bang in front of the front door. The noise aroused the owner who came downstairs in his pyjamas, hair dishevelled and still half asleep to open the front door and find BP facing him with a man stood on his shoulders, painting.

'What on earth is going on?' demanded the owner and BP's answer was, 'Have you got the money, Mush?'

A record try scorer at the old Bramley club and a real character is BP.

HENDERSON GILL

Hendy moved from Bradford Northern to Rochdale Hornets then on to Wigan and that is where I met up with him. The most likeable of kids, Hendy brought a ray of sunshine to the dressing room and always, always, played with a smile on his face! A strong runner, he was another quicker-than-he-looked wingman, quite capable of scoring long distance tries and he developed into a reliable left-footed goal kicker.

When we first worked together though, I found him a little hard to handle. The turning point was one cold winters evening when Hendy turned up for training with the 'posse', a tough looking group of around five Afro-Brits from Huddersfield!

'Now then lads are you hungry?' I asked them, 'because we have some beans on toast upstairs in the players' canteen and there are some spare.' I made five mates for life, plus Hendy. But earlier in the season he had arrived very late for training and as the squad had almost finish their programme, I told Hendy to get some laps of the field done. As we were having our beans on toast up in the canteen, one of the lads was looking down onto the pitch and said, 'Hey, Maurice, there is someone running around the field.' I looked and it was Hendy, I had forgotten him and he must have done a hundred laps. I went down and brought him in and as he tucked into his beans on toast, he flashed that big smile and said, 'It was great running, Maurice, I enjoyed it.'

A great team man our Hendy.

4

CENTRES

PHIL LARDER

Phil may be better known as a coach of Great Britain, Widnes, Keighley Cougars and Sheffield Eagles, and later as the 'Guru' of defensive coaches in rugby union. But he was, for many years, a very good centre at Oldham and Whitehaven. He was also an excellent goal-kicker and several times kicked over 100 goals in a season.

Coming from a rugby league background in Oldham, Phil paid the penalty of being clever at school by winning a place at Loughborough College and becoming a teacher! Then playing rugby union at college he joined the Sale club and gained county recognition when selected for Lancashire. But the old game called and he signed for the 'Roughyeds' at the old Watersheddings, Oldham, to begin a long association with the 13-a-side game, ending as a player up in Cumbria.

Phil then became the head of the National Rugby League Coaching Scheme and I worked with him as his Yorkshire regional coach. When I was appointed the Great Britain coach in 1984 I asked Phil if he would join me as assistant coach at national level and he agreed. With the very experienced Les Bettinson as the team manager, and drafting in Mike Stabler as team physio, we set about the daunting task of turning around our international sides fortunes following the disastrous tour down under in 1984, where we were beaten in all six Test matches against the Aussies and Kiwis.

We turned the Kiwi part a bit with a hard-fought drawn series in 1985 but the wheels came off in '86 when we were beaten by the fabulous 'Unbeatables' at Old Trafford and Elland Road, by big scores. We prepared for the final Test at Central Park, Wigan in November 1986 with a week's camp at the Shaw Hill golf complex, at Chorley and here is the start of a very strange occurrence.

As something different I organised a presentation of the team's playing jerseys on the last team meeting on the Friday before Saturday's game. Each player was advised not to forget their jersey the following day when we left our camp for Central Park and each one answered as their name was called to come to the head of the class to collect the precious jersey amid applause from their team mates. Very emotional indeed and a thing that all the players remember to this day.

Now in the previous season we had played the Kiwis and the spare jerseys from the kit were presented to the manager, the two coaches and the physio – four spare jerseys in all – the Kiwi kit being identical to the Aussie kit apart from the identification lettering, i.e. v New Zealand, 1985 above the lion's head logo over the heart.

Came the day, and, despite checking that all the kit was in place, on arrival at Wigan's dressing rooms we found that Chris Burton had left his number 11 jersey at Shaw Hill. We were only 45 minutes away from kick-off and in no way could we have recovered the jersey in time for the start.

In this Test match, inexplicably there were no numbers on the spare kit, unlike in the Kiwi series when the spares had four various numbers on the backs. Panic gripped us but enter Phil Larder, and this is absolutely true. Opening his bag he produced his spare jersey from the Kiwi series, still in the polythene bag, in mint condition, and on the back was number 11, The only difference between Phil's jersey and the rest was the very small 'v New Zealand, 1985' above the lion's head, unnoticeable to anyone.

We thought it was an omen from the great coach in the sky, but to no avail. We still lost, albeit by a very small margin.

Phil has certainly been a good omen to English rugby union and my old friend is the benchmark for all defensive coaches, and most of them hail from a League background: Joe Lydon, Shaun Edwards, Ellery Hanley, Mick Ford and David Ellis, who all followed Phil onto the world stage of international rugby union and all have made a big impact with their defensive qualities. I wonder if they all carry spare jerseys in their kit bag?

Well done Phil old mate, you certainly got the England mob to 'hit, lift and drive' in those tackles,

ANONYMOUS

Again the reason for this book is not to ridicule anyone but this particular story is to lay to rest the myth once and for all that the lack of brain power is not peculiar to props and hookers! Some backs too are not the sharpest tool in the box as highlighted by a current Super League player who was on Featherstone Rovers' books a few seasons ago.

'Fev' were going through a lean spell when suddenly they found their form with a cracking win, at the old Post Office Road, over a side at the top of the division. After which, the players were ecstatic and to a man decided to go out on the town on a much needed bonding session.

Now the players' car park at the ground had had a spate of car break-ins and the board of directors had laid out a substantial sum to make the car park harder to get in and out of than Fort Knox. And the groundsman locked the players' car park up tight at 8:00pm prompt after matches.

Well our anonymous centre lived in the Dewsbury area of the county, so come 10:30pm, and all in good spirits, one of the players said to him, 'Hey up, it's half past ten and the car park is locked at 8:00, you're in for the night.'

So our intrepid back said 'It's OK, I'll climb over the fence to get my car.' Amid roars of laughter from his team mates. One of the props said, 'But you can't get out you plank.'

'Oh yea, I see now.' said Mr. Anonymous, and I thought forwards were supposed to be a bit slow!

PETER ANSON

Tolstoy would have struggled to relate all the stories surrounding this wonderful character who was a product of the old Hunslet district of Leeds. Now there are those that say Leeds was a district of Hunslet, these are Hunslet lads of course, but it would be totally unfair of anyone writing about the good old days of our game without spending time describing the immense part this heavily industrialised area played in creating the folklore and superb traditions of our much loved game.

In a district that produced tens of larger than life characters per terraced street, and there were hundreds and hundreds of terraced streets, the late and sadly missed Peter Anson must rate with the highest.

'Anno' or as I remember him, 'Peter', played as a professional for several clubs: Keighley, Batley and Dewsbury, but his first love was playing, as a young man for his local club Hunslet at the old Parkside ground.

Peter played the game for many years after his professional days and was still as tough a competitor when he moved from the centre into the pack. As an amateur he played for teams in the Hunslet area, firstly Coghlans, an engineering works team then to the strong Bisons side that played from the pre-cast concrete company at Stourton.

I played both with and against Peter over the years. With him at Dewsbury for a season and against him for a couple of seasons when I played for Burton Sports. The Bisons v

Burtons matches in the Leeds and District League were tough games with little to choose between the sides. But I remember Peter sitting beside me on the bus taking the Dewsbury team to play Hull at the Boulevard, who were a hard side with a renowned pack.

'We must stand up to their pack today Maurice,' he said, and proceeded to tell me a piece of his homespun philosophy, 'even if they hit us with the grandstand, it doesn't hurt forever and we'll get over it.'

Another tale is of when Bisons had fought their way to the Yorkshire Cup final against Hull Ambassador at the old Tattersfield ground at Doncaster. The Hull side had a big, tough prop who had been warned of hard case Peter Anson and it was his intention to test Peter out early to see how tough he was!

As the teams took the field the tough prop called over to the Bisons team, 'Which one of you is Anson?'

Peter got to the tough prop in the first six tackles and BANG, out like a light. As they were carrying the prop off, Peter bent over the stretcher, looked into the props eyes, just as he had come round and said, 'I am'.

I always thought Peter had a look of Kirk Douglas the film star, just something about him, but Kirk could not have been as tough as Peter. The question inevitably asked when any team played Coghlans or Bisons was, 'Is Anson playing today?' No greater compliment could be paid to any player. He was, and is, a Hunslet legend, Peter Anson.

CHRIS ARKWRIGHT

A St Helens lad, son and grandson of good rugby league players, Jack, the grandad and young Jack, the son. Chris's dad, young Jack, was a big, tough front rower for Warrington and granddad Jack was the big fearsome Great Britain and

Warrington second rower who, with his Warrington team mate, prop forward Johnny Miller, put the fear of the good lord up the Aussies on the 1936 tour.

Now Chris could have fitted in anywhere but I've included him in the centre because this little tale happened while he was playing in that position for me in international football for Great Britain. The St Helens utility player was selected to go on the 1984 tour but was injured shortly before the team flew out and was unable to make the trip. His club form prior to the 1985 Kiwi series was excellent and I selected him as substitute for the first Test at Headingley against a New Zealand side that were arguably the best in the world, having recently beaten the all-conquering Australians.

In that match Great Britain scored a memorable try when, with little time to play and the Kiwis leading by two points, Des Drummond picked up a kick through on his own try line and made a 25 yard break and passed to Deryck Fox, who transferred the ball immediately to Chris Arkwright. Chris ran diagonally for what seemed an age before passing to Ellery Hanley who burst down the touchline and gave an inside pass to Joe Lydon who strode to the posts for an outstanding try. Joe also converted and with a few minutes to play we had a three point lead. Unfortunately the great Kiwi side scored in the final seconds, kicked the goal and we lost by two points, creditable, but a loss all the same.

In the dressing room after the game I spoke to Chris about his part in that superb try. 'I just wondered Chris why you ran so far across field and seemed to be looking up into the stand,' I asked.

His answer was as honest as the day is long, 'As I got the ball Maurice, I noticed a beautiful young lady sat in the stand and I was looking at her and almost forgot to pass to Ellery, as I was trying to attract her attention.'

What can you say to that, and he wasn't kidding. I don't

know what Grandad Jack would have had to say!

JOE LYDON

'Hollywood' Joe I used to call him. Good looking, suave, well educated and a bloody good player! His magnificent try in the first Australian Test at Old Trafford in 1986, when he took a wide pass some 80 yards out and proceeded to out run the Aussie cover and round the excellent defender, Gary Jack, in great style to dive over majestically, will stay in my memory forever.

Joe had a superb career at Widnes and Wigan before going into coaching at Central Park and later being included in the top class England Rugby Union Coaching and Youth Development set up, specialising in the Sevens worldwide competitions as England coach.

Another memory of mine is of going as an after-dinner speaker to various functions, in Yorkshire, Lancashire and Cumbria and finding each time in my bread roll a neat, clean note which read, 'Hi Maurice, it's me again, Joe.'

I learnt years later when speaking at a dinner in Lancashire that Joe would suss out where I was speaking and with his network of mates always found one who would be at that particular dinner who would then locate my seat on the top table and slip the note neatly into my bread roll. What a man, 'Hollywood' Joe Lydon! Nice kid.

5

STAND-OFFS

NORMAN SMITH

Norman played at stand-off for Dewsbury in the 1960s and went on to coach at the club twice and at Headingley as the A team coach and assistant coach. He was also the very successful Milford player/coach, then coach to the Leeds amateur club when his playing days were over. He later came to Bramley with me as my A team captain in 1975 and was an excellent stand-off and a very good coach.

It was on his debut for Dewsbury at Barrow that Norman first came face to face with Frank Foster. Big Frank was player/coach at Craven Park when this story happened thus.

Norman was on substitute duty and when the Dewsbury team were out on the pitch, warming up before Barrow came out, coach Tommy Smales asked Norman to nip back into the dressing room and bring the substitutes' number cards as he had left them in there by mistake. Norman found the numbers and was on his way back out to the team when he heard the sound of studs on the concrete passage floor and realised that the Barrow team were on their way out to the field, so he decided to wait until the Barrow lads had passed by.

Norman bobbed his head out of the doorway and glanced up the passage to get his first glimpse of the fearsome Frank Foster, complete with face covered in Vaseline and looking immense in his blue and white striped jersey, striding out in front of his team to do battle with the visitors from Yorkshire.

As Frank reached the doorway in which Norman was cowering, he stopped dead in his tracks and all the Barrow team bumped into him without Frank moving an inch. Looking straight at the shivering debutant, Frank, in his rich Cumbria dialect said, 'It's a long way to come for losing money, marra.' and led his team into the arena.

Norman tells the tale with pride that Frank Foster actually spoke to him. It took Norman a week off work to get over the trauma.

Another tale involving Norman, and my old mate Peter Jarvis, whom we will hear more about later, occurred on a coaching course at the National Sports Centre, Lilleshall. Now at the time I was a regional coach, down on the course as staff with those wonderful coaches, the superb late Laurie Gant and the late, great, Albert Fearnley.

It was Thursday evening and the Laws of the Game examination always took place on Thursdays as the field tests were on the final day, Friday. The lecture theatre was the venue for the Laws exam and it was my turn to be in charge to make sure everything went by the book, as it was important that the course was fair and straight down the line.

I greeted the candidates, and made sure they were all seated about four seats apart and staggered to avoid any copying taking place. I advised them that they had two hours to complete the questionnaire and, on finishing the test, would they quietly put their papers on my desk and leave as quietly as possible, so not to distract the other candidates.

'Your time starts now,' I told them and clicked on the stop watch. Silence descended. Only the slight scratching of pen on paper was heard as the students' brains creaked under the weight of use!

On the hour both Norman and Peter Jarvis finished simultaneously and both crept down to the floor of the theatre to deposit their test papers together. With a wink and a silent wave they departed to the bar.

As there was still a lot of time to go, I thought I would check and mark both sets of tests and opened them up. The answer to question one was 'Yes', both had 'Yes'. Question two was 'No' and again both had 'No'. I got a shock when I read question three for Norman had 'I don't know' and Peter had 'Neither do I'. Both insisted it must have been telepathy and to this day I can't understand it. They wouldn't stoop to cheating, would they?

On the same course were a group of lads from the Milford wanting to qualify and a guy called Mike Workman from the Mitre Company, who as a sponsorship were giving away free boots, kit bags and tee shirts to all the students. Unfortunately Mike broke his ankle during a session of touch and pass and the Milford lads carried Mike, in agony, from the playing fields up to the Hall. As they carried him the first thing the Milford lads asked him was not, 'How are you Mike,' but, 'We are still in for that gear, aren't we mush?'

Mercenary or what! (They did get the gear.)

DICKY WILLIAMS

Please forgive me if I now drift into a spot of self-indulgent nostalgia, as we go back to immediately after the Second World War to recall a hero of mine from those wonderfully simple days when stand-offs made play for their centres, who, in turn, made openings for their wing partners.

Dicky Williams was one of eight Welshmen who played for the Leeds club in the cup run of 1947. Gareth Price and TL (Les) Williams were the centres with Tommy Cornelious on the right wing and Dicky at number 6. The master footballer Dai Jenkins was a scrum half and the two men responsible for winning the ball from the scrum were Dai Prosser and Con Murphy, as Welsh as they come. The eighth

Welshman was the peerless Isaac Andrew (Ike) Owens, the fastest loose forward of his day.

Some good judges, my Great Britain manager and former player and coach of the Red Devils, Salford, Les Bettinson, in particular, reckons that the demise of our international fortunes came about when we stopped the supply of the top Welsh backs that graced our game since the breakaway in the middle 1890s, the last real top stand-off to 'come north' being Jonathan Davies.

Dicky Williams, he of the wavy ginger hair and twinkling feet, the dummy and acceleration, the side-step into the clear and the perfectly timed pass to send the support over, the copybook tackles around the ankles, had it all. His greatest achievement was to captain the 1954 touring side after being a member of the 1950 tour and his move from the Leeds club, to arch rivals and near neighbours Hunslet in the early 1950s, caused a major stir within the city.

Dicky's opponents at stand-off on a regular basis in those days read like a Who's Who of all time greats, and connoisseurs of the game had the time of their lives as the brilliant, skilful stand-offs clashed each week and punters paid hard earned money to be entertained and dazzled by the likes of Dicky, Willie Horn (Barrow), Cec Mountford (Wigan), Willie Davies (Bradford Northern) and Ray Price (Warrington). And there were other middle backs who could move between centre and stand-off, Bryn Knowelden (Barrow), Jacky Cunliffe (Wigan), Lewis Jones (Leeds) and possibly the best pure uncapped stand-off of his time, Brian Gabbitas (Hunslet). All wonderful, constructive players followed shortly by Dave Bolton (Wigan), Harry Archer (Workington Town) and the fabulous Alex Murphy (Saints).

Thanks for the memories and here's to the next batch of world beating stand-off halves, or are they a dying breed?

GLEN KNIGHT

If ever a player did not fulfil his potential, then Glen Knight is the one. A superb all round footballer with handling, kicking and tactical skills in abundance. His reading of a game was uncanny and he could carry out the coach's instructions to the letter.

He had big club experience as he did the rounds a bit, playing at Castleford, where he made the first team at a very early age and was one of the many good footballers produced in the Castleford nursery under the expert guidance of ace coach, John Sheriden, then Oldham and Warrington, where Glen was bought by the great Alex Murphy to build up the 'Wire' prestige and strengthen the back line, and Huddersfield, where I coached him for a spell.

One of Glen's problems was that he had no 'middle'. He was high or low, good or bad, brilliant or terrible, there was no 'not too bad' with Glen, no middle. On his day, he was international class, but two minutes later, as bad as bad gets!

Now in a tale involving Glen, a good young Kiwi, Mick Punter, and a man we will discuss at length later, Peter Clarke, I will delve briefly into the all important facet of man management required by any coach at any level of life.

Huddersfield were playing the then New Hunslet, at Fartown and young Punter, who had joined us from the Glenora club in Auckland, was on his debut.

Peter Clarke was a case-hardened old pro, a hooker his entire career and a tough, well respected battler who was as hard as they come.

Glen was his brilliant best in the first twenty minutes and his expertise allowed our team to take a 20 points to nil lead and Punter, who was at scrum half to Glen's stand-off, to have a cracking first twenty.

Then, the switch-off by Glen and his inconsistency cost us 18 points and made Punter look ordinary. Half-time could not come quickly enough for me to get the team into the dressing room. My cap and coat were thrown into a corner and I had Glen sitting in the first seat near the door, then Punter and at the side of him, the hard man, Clarkey.

'What's the matter now Glen?' I demanded of him.

'I don't know, I can't seem to be able to get into the game,' he whined.

I explained that he had been in the game in the first twenty minutes and he had all but won the match for us.

'I don't know what's wrong, I seem to have lost my concentration,' moaned Glen.

All this time, Punter had been seeing this English style coach/player relationship for the very first time in his life and he was open mouthed, watching bemused. I knew I had to do something quick to snap the team back into life, 'Well get the bloody thing back, and fast' I shouted and gave Glen a big flat handed slap across his face, and to bring Punter back to the land of the living, I gave him a swift back-hander across the chops too.

Now the man management part, as I moved along the row of players, Clarkey, the tough nut, leaned back in his seat, folded his arms and very, very slowly shook his head. I leant forward, gently slapped his knee and said, 'Bloody good half Peter,' man management, simply man management!

Poor old Knighty. As I said, he could lift you high then drop you quick, but he knew the game inside-out and we often discussed various set plays, Glen and I, as he was a player who could have a big input for a coach who would use his know-how.

In 1980 our Huddersfield team reached the semi-final of the old Yorkshire Cup and took a very good Leeds side all the way at Headingley, loosing by only four points in a cracking game.

Because of a couple of injuries the previous week, I asked Glen to play a one-off at full-back in the semi-final and he agreed, although he did have reservations about standing in as last line of defence against the best pair of club wingmen at that time, Alan Smith and John Atkinson, both test wingers and both great players.

'Glen,' I told him, 'I have the utmost faith in you, just be careful of Smith's strength near the touchline and Atky's pace as he comes in and goes out, and don't forget, you are doing me a favour and if it doesn't work, we will never mention it again'.

Well, after about two minutes, Smith was released down the touchline and he barrelled his way passed Glen to score a very good try and to Glen's credit he went on to have a good game, almost winning it for us in the final seconds when he strode clear down the centre of the field and was caught just short after a superb 60 yard run.

The footnote is that whenever I see him I immediately mention that first tackle on Alan Smith and Glen always says, 'You promised never to mention it'.

Glen went into coaching and indeed secured a good job in France and I often wondered if he used my slapping technique in the dressing room.

Glen Knight, when on song, brilliant!

BARRY LANGTON

Either number six or seven, Barry was a player that went down on your team sheet, one of the first. I coached him at the Stanningley amateur club when a load of cracking young players came to us from the Bramley Rugby Union Club. There were about six joined us and almost all went into professional rugby, amongst them, Terry Langton, Barry's younger brother, who was my scrum-half at Halifax as well as at the amateur club.

Barry was a cheeky little sod and his favourite type of tackle was the old 'Cumbrian' throw. Timing and strength were the key factors of this devastating tackle when the ball carrier tried to hand off with his free arm, the tackler grabbed the arm, thrust his leg in front of the ball carrier and threw him ju-jitsu style over his leg. The tackled player went down face first into the mud with nothing to stop himself as he was holding the ball with his other arm and BANG, face in to the dirt! A horrific tackle and Barry was a master at it.

The cheeky stand-off preferred big men to work it on and they came no bigger than Jim Mills when the giant, hard man prop was playing at Workington Town and they came down to play at McLaren Field. Barry did a job on big Jim and the ground shuddered as the international prop hit the dirt, as described, face first.

Jim bounced up, 'You little b******, I'll break your neck,' he shouted.

'You'll have to catch me first,' called Barry and Jim chased him all around the field, about two yards behind the quick, cheeky little half-back until things quietened down.

Terry was once incarcerated in Blackpool 'nick' for being drunk and disorderly on a Stanningley end of season trip. Barry, in a similar state as their kid, bought a Monopoly game set so that he could use the 'Get Out of Jail Free' card to give to the desk sergeant at the 'nick' to get their kid out, and Barry finished up in the next cell.

Don't ever let Barry Langton give you the Cumbrian throw, avoid it at all costs!

6

SCRUM-HALVES

ALF BURNELL

The game of Rugby League Football produces characters mainly because of its tough, no-nonsense Northern traditions; play hard, play to win, give a knock, take a knock.

The background of our game was the pit-head and the foundry floor, the mill-block and the building site. The old adage that you don't have to be of giant stature to play the game follows the old saying 'They don't make diamonds as big as coal-bricks'. Hence we think of half-backs as small, thick set, nuggety men, quick to anger and tough as old boots.

In most cases that was, and indeed is, so. But the scrum-half also is usually thought of as a crafty, all-knowing, streetwise animal, up to all sorts of devious tricks and a player who is jealously guarded by his bigger, rougher team mates, the forwards.

There always have been though some half-backs that did not require protection from their forwards, they could look after themselves – Tommy Bishop (St Helens), Andy Gregory (Wigan) and Kevin Dick (Leeds) are three fire-brands that spring to mind and before them, Herbert Goodfellow (Wakefield Trinity), Dai Jenkins (Leeds) and Tommy McCue (Widnes), who made two tours ten years apart in 1936 and 1946.

One of the toughest scrum-halves when I was a kid was Hunslet's own Alf Burnell. With his shock of red hair

'Ginger' Burnell came from the iron hard stock of Hunslet, rugby league's heartland. His brother Don, played for Yorkshire as a scrum-half and all the Burnell brothers played the game at some level or other.

Alf toured in 1954 and the other half-back on the trip was that gem of a player, Gerry Helme (Warrington), an all time great. Alf was a strong, stand up, knock 'em over player who would not, and could not, take a backward step. He was from a district that did not take backward steps.

Later in life, as a cracking landlord, Alf would hold court and relate hilarious tales about his career in rugby and one was about the time he joined the navy as a kid at the time of the Second World War. Alf was placed in HM Submarines and after training was posted to Singapore. Alf's sub arrived on the day Singapore fell to the Japanese and all the crew were taken prisoner of war and put into Changi jail on the island.

Soon their tropical whites were in tatters and all that remained of the proud uniform was the shoulder flashing 'HM Submarines'. One evening a guard came around to tell the prisoners that they must wash all uniforms, no matter how tattered they may be, and be on parade at six o'clock the following morning as a very important visitor was inspecting them. 'You must be spick and span, or else,' warned the guard.

So at six prompt the guards hustled the prisoners into line and Alf, with his shock of flame coloured hair was placed bang in the front line, dead opposite the front gate.

It was ten o'clock when the gates swung open, and with the sun beating down, five Rolls Royce state cars drove slowly into the jail square, slap bang in front of Alf! A red carpet was rolled out to the middle car and a neatly uniformed officer marched to the car door, opened it and out stepped the 'God King' himself, Hirohito, Emperor of Japan.

Every man on parade bowed low, as they had been told to do, as did all the guards. The Emperor walked slowly up the red carpet and right up to Alf. Hirohito stopped in front of our Hunslet hero and, looking at the flashings, so bright in the sunlight, said, 'Ah, His Majesty's Submarines'.

Alf bowed and said 'Yes, your majesty'.

Hirohito weighed Alf up with a long glance and said, 'Where are you from?'

Alf stiffened with pride and after bowing low said, 'Hunslet your Majesty,' glowing just thinking of home.

'Ah, yes,' said Hirohito, 'Hunslet, all four cups 1907–08'.

The one and only Alf Burnell.

WILLIE JOHNSON

My very good friend and my old scrum-half from my last coaching spell at Dewsbury. Willie is a St Helens lad and played mainly for Clock Face in St Helens as an amateur but also had years in the professional game at Swinton, Rochdale Hornets, Mansfield Marksmen, Nottingham Outlaws and Dewsbury.

Willie has coached since he retired at Leigh and Swinton. I signed Willie from Nottingham and he turned out to be one of my best signings ever. Brave as a bobbin, honest as the day is long and a very knowledgeable footballer and drop goal expert.

Willie was knocking on a bit when I signed him but believing in the old saying, 'if you're good enough, you're young enough', I thankfully went through with the deal.

At half-time in one game against Runcorn Highfield, we were behind against a side we should have beaten easily and having several 'elder statesmen' in the side I thought I would gee them up a bit so I put the question to the whole team, 'Give me a show of hands, how many of you are over 32 years old?'

I knew that Willie was at least 34 but the crafty little bugger kept his hand down, although the other four players who were over that age owned up to it.

The ploy of a veiled threat over ages worked and we won by a clear 30 points, but I was surprised Willie had not owned up to the fact of his being over 32. So I pulled him in the tea room after the match, 'What's up Willie, why didn't you admit to being over 32 at half-time?' I asked.

'32' said Willie, 'I thought you said 42' and he turned away, smiling. He wasn't smiling when I got to him after a drawn cup tie at St Helens, when a drop goal would have won the cup tie for us and put us in the quarter-final, but with only minutes to play we had 18 consecutive tackles in the Saints' 20-metre area and Willie, whom I had given strict instructions to drop as many goals as he could, ignored my orders. I called him all the little devils I could think of, but would I sign him again, you bet I would, he was a belter!

KEN LOXTON

I have coached a hell of a lot of players over the years, internationals, county and just ordinary club men, and have been asked many times, 'Who was the best player you have worked with?' I've thought about this question long and hard, but the answer I come up with every time is Ken Loxton.

Why? Well it's easier telling his worse points than his good ones. He wasn't over big, was in fact one of the slowest runners I ever coached, he had his own mind set, he could be a pain in the bum, rarely made a break and he was one of the worst kickers of a ball I've ever seen.

So what made him so bloody good? Well, he never missed one tackle while he played for me. Added to which, if our forwards scored say 60 tries in a season 'Locky' would have made 58 of them with passes that even I could have scored from.

He should have been awarded Rugby League's VC for bravery on the field of play. He set himself up, time and again, match after match, season after season, to be crunched in heavy tackles only for the tackler to find Ken didn't have the ball – it was being planted down for a try after being slipped away with sleight of hand like a magician.

Ken has stayed on the field in key matches when a normal man would have retired hurt. His shuffling gait and exaggerated dummies belied the skill that manipulated such deft passes that opened up defences for years in the game.

He was the key figure, amongst some massive key figures, that turned Halifax away from an unreturnable abyss in the late 1970s. It showed his style when he was selected, on merit, to represent Great Britain in front of the all time great Alex Murphy, against New Zealand in 1971 and the tries he manufactured during his time at Huddersfield are legendary.

But it was at the match involving me and the Blue Dragon at Cardiff that was Ken's swan song when a severe back injury forced his retirement from the game he had served with such courage and distinction. In that game at Ninian Park, as well as coach, I was acting physio and had to attend to Ken as he writhed in agony with a displaced vertebra. Luckily for Ken's sake the Cardiff team doctor was the top man at the local hospital and he phoned through to have a theatre ready for Ken when the ambulance arrived.

Later Ken coached at Halifax and at Featherstone Rovers but his skills on the pitch are the reasons that I consider the Normanton lad something very special in the game.

ANONYMOUS

I suppose the bush Aussies, the ones who live way out in the wilderness, on a cattle farm or working as a cane cutter at the top end up in North Queensland, are just as rough and tough a bunch of men you could meet anywhere.

Well this little tale centres on the old Bramley club in the 1970s when the chairman and his board of directors were gentlemen of the old school who would stand no nonsense from either players or coaches. They were straight in everything they did, usually very clean and smartly dressed men with impeccable manners and a church-going attitude towards all things physically clean and tidy, to the extent that even to accidentally break wind in their presence was taboo.

Then here enters an Aussie, from as far north in Australia as can keep their feet dry, asking for a trial run with the club and as we were a bit thin on the ground for scrum-halves I agreed.

He looked OK in training and as we had an A team game up in Cumbria on the weekend, I put him in.

Now like all clubs in the lower reaches we at Bramley had to watch the pennies and, in those days, getting a bus for away games with the A team was a treat and only top professional soccer clubs travelled on a bus that had a toilet. We had the obligatory bucket on the back seat, only in case one had had a little too much to drink and for that reason only!

So off we went on the long, long trip to the North West along the recently completed M62 and onto the M6, which at the time did not have as many service stations as today and, in some instances, one had to travel twice or three times the distance than today's 20 odd miles.

There was a particularly large turnout of the board for this long trek, unusual too because the A team did not attract so many, especially on such a long haul but there they were, chairman, vice chairman, A team director, four board members and the club secretary, all in their normal seats at the front of the bus.

We had just passed the last services for many miles when our new and unknown Aussie, who had been playing cards in a school, mid-bus, suddenly called to me, 'Morrie, I need the toilet, bad, ask him to stop the bus and I'll nip behind the bushes'.

I went to the driver and whispered in his ear, 'Can we stop for a second while our Aussie nips to the loo?'

'What, and risk my livelihood? Not on your life. Tell him he'll have to wait.'

I relayed the bad news to the Aussie, who after about another five minutes was going red in the face.

'Mate' he said, 'I've only the one pair of pants with me and there is no way I can mess them up, pass me the bucket!'

The North Queenslander planted the bucket in centre isle and the team around him dispersed quickly to positions as far away as possible from the crouching Aussie and sat in deathly silence awaiting the probable outcome. To make matters worse, because of the winter conditions outside, the rear heaters were blowing down the bus, towards the unaware board members at the front of the saloon.

Suddenly and quietly, like the poison gas of the First World War, the aroma struck. Eight startled faces slowly turned around in unison, as if being pulled on the same string and each of the directors gasped in horror as they were confronted by our new Aussie, squat, trousers around his ankles, smiling at them, then winking cheekily, as the board, with cries of, 'disgusting, outrageous' and 'This has never happened on our bus before' and 'Driver, for God's sake turn that heater off!' proceeded to hold an extraordinary board meeting to decide the fate of the unfortunate Antipodean.

The Chairman rose from his seat and waving his arm, like Moses parting the Red Sea, he commanded, 'Stop this bus and remove the Australian,' sounding just like Charlton Heston in the *Ten Commandments*.

I asked, 'Remove to where, Chairman?'

'Anywhere, but get him off this saloon.' answered the club

leader, and the bus pulled onto the hard shoulder, the Aussie alighted and was never seen again.

But as we drove onto the motorway again, one of the players called down the bus, 'Who's going to empty the bucket?'

The question was never answered from the board and the aroma had to be suffered for the remainder of the trip up country.

If the Aussie ever reads this, please get in touch for old times' sake.

7

PROP FORWARDS

PETER JARVIS

Peter has a had a mention already in the tale of the mystery of the Lilleshall tests with Norman Smith but it is as an individual that 'Jarvy' shines.

A big lad, Jarvy and I moved around together in the days of the competitive scrum when the ball winning abilities of an open side prop were crucial to you having the ball during a game or not having it.

Jarvy could get it for you as well as being the old-fashioned front rower who would cart the ball up all day and make a nuisance of himself in defence around the play-the-ball area. He was very streetwise too, as his day job demanded, because he was a pub landlord and was the youngest, at 21, on Joshua Tetley's books, being the boss in the famous old drinking pub in the centre of Leeds, The Whip.

I joined forces with Jarvy at Bramley, and then our partnership continued at Bradford Northern, Halifax, Huddersfield then back to Bramley where Jarvy was my colts coach. He and I worked together in the National Coaching Scheme too when, along with a fine bunch of coaches, we organised the Yorkshire Area for the scheme and ran courses for coaches, children and adults.

But one tale epitomises Jarvy's will to win and his ruthlessness to achieve that win.

Training one winter's evening at the old Thrum Hall

ground at Halifax, we had a big, strong player on trial from the successful Dewsbury Celtic amateur side. I had given the squad a short game of touch and pass and this big kid hits Jarvy with a glancing blow with his elbow. I saw Jarvy's face, and knowing him, realised that the young man was in danger. Even though he was at fault for attacking Jarvy as he did, I pulled Jarvy and told him to leave it out as taking retribution would do no-one any good.

The snow was falling and the trialist accidentally received a cut head and was taken to Halifax hospital to be stitched. Now Jarvy always said that he was not responsible for the cut head and what followed supports his plea.

We had finished training as the snow had developed into one of those Pennine blizzards that we used to get back then and the trialist still had not returned from hospital and his clothes were still on his dressing peg. Jarvy's will to win came to the fore when he was ready to leave for home for he grabbed the big tin of Ralgex, the deep heat odourless ointment, which was a killer if applied to the nether regions of the body, and daubed the lad's underpants, back and front with the killer potion.

The following training night the kid told me what had happened when he arrived back from the hospital and we had all left for home. Because of the blizzard the kid wanted to be on his way and forsaking the shower he dressed quickly and ploughed through the deep snow to his car, blasted the heater on to full and directed it onto his body as well as onto the windscreen, it was then that he felt a tingling sensation around his nether regions. By the time he had gone 100 yards he was driving with the car door open, trying to get some relief to his red hot groin. Another 100 yards and the car was stopped and the kid was out in the blizzard stuffing snow down his under-pants.

'I can't understand what it was,' the kid told me as Jarvy

passed us.

The big man leaned over and said something quietly to the kid. It sounded like a warning not to mess with Jarvy. He never did again!

At Huddersfield together some time later Jarvy was doing a great job for me with the younger players as he was a great dressing room character. I used to get the players in to the ground for a run out on the morning of the match but the groundsman had a big say with the directors and he refused to allow us on the field on the morning of the game if it was wet.

As it always pays to be in with the groundsman we did as he requested, at least when he was around but this particular morning he was in his bed so I took the team onto the field. To end the session I had the pack practice a bit of scrimmaging against the backs and when we finished the area we had used was a mess, all churned up.

We were in a spot of bother as we had no roller to level out the morass, but Jarvy came to the rescue. The big man was weighing in around 18 to 19 stones so he just laid on the ground and all the players rolled him over and over to leave a perfectly flat and repaired field – I always knew he would be of some use some day!

Jarvy went from colts coach at Bramley to first team coach at the club when I moved on from McLaren Field and no coach has had a job so close to home as he was then landlord of the pub that was actually in the ground at Bramley, The Villager.

I mentioned Jarvy being a character. Well the comical side of his character was the ability to murder the English language with what became known as 'Jarvyisms'.

One of his classics was when delivering a team talk at half-time and he wanted to stress the need to work harder. 'I've been watching the video of our last game,' he said to the forwards, 'and you two back three aren't getting about enough.'

Another team talk about a certain area of play he ended with 'And that's what happens. That's hitting the hammer on the head!'

One of the players said, 'Nail Peter,' and Jarvy replied 'And the nail as well.'

On a coaching course at Cowley School, St Helens, Jarvy was asked to give an example, other than touch and pass, as a warm-up game before actual training. 'I give my lads a game of that Garlic Football that they play in Ireland.'

Another Hunslet lad to the core, Peter Jarvis was out of professional football when I was contacted by a wealthy gentleman builder, Mr Jack Lunn, who had joined the Hunslet board and wanted a coach that had the club at heart and could do well for them. I recommended Jarvy strongly and he got the job, but on merit. He had the good sense to bring in David Ward as his assistant coach and, between the two very talented men, they pushed their team into the division's championship final, only to be beaten by Swinton at Old Trafford. Back into junior football he went and revitalised the fortunes of the Milford Marlins club in Leeds, ending with a spell as director of rugby at the progressive amateur side and was at the club when they upgraded their set-up to introduce a wonderful sports centre which caters for all sports in the Kirkstall area of the city.

Director of rugby, who would have thought my old mate would have risen to those dizzy heights? Not bad for a prop. Another super kid, Jarvy.

ROY DICKINSON

Big Roy Dickinson, one of the most humorous men in a

game of top comics to ever grace the game. Big and blonde, always a smile on his face, as tough as old boots and always a pleasure to meet, Roy was well respected throughout a long and distinguished career.

His clubs included Leeds, Halifax and Bramley and after retiring was seen regularly in The Villager in the company of his mate, Peter Jarvis. It would have been a very brave man who caused any trouble in that establishment with those two behind the bar!

The fact that Roy and Peter were big mates strengthens the old true story that in our game you could knock seven bells out of an opponent and still be mates after the game. I don't mean 'handbags at three paces', I mean go to town, fair and square and knock hell out of your mate, because, make no mistake, he was going to knock hell out of you given half a chance. That was, and I dare say, is the nature of the game.

Peter was playing for me in the Yorkshire Cup semi-final against Leeds at Headingley in 1980 and was pitted against big Roy. We knew that if we let Leeds dictate the game they would murder us, so we had to start on the offensive and maintain that attitude as long as possible, throughout the game if we could.

I covered this particular game and some of the issues involved in the Glen Knight saga, but the punishing runs of big Roy had to be nullified if we were to do well. I mentioned this to Peter in passing and he replied with a knowledgeable wink and that was that.

From the kick-off the ball went to Roy and Peter arrived at the same time. Peter caught Roy on his way up in the jump for the kick and with a tremendous tackle, tipped Roy in the air and landed on top of him with all his almost 19 stones and with a resounding thud.

Roy was knocked out, he had dislocated his shoulder and broken a rib and the big lad was in a bad state as one can imagine. Roy was helped off and took no further part in this game, nor in any other for a good eight weeks. No boasting from Peter, he just got on with his part of the game plan and held the simple philosophy that the same thing could happen to anyone playing this game. Big Roy held the same thought that it goes with the game, good times and bad, no injuries for a long time then one crops up. That's rugby league.

Although Roy never shirked a thing on the field and was noted for never taking a backward step in life, he would be the first to admit to not being a prolific try scorer. In truth he didn't score many. His area of expertise was carting the ball up and knocking the other bloke sideways, this he did with a vengeance.

I coached him at both Leeds and at Bramley, and indeed for Great Britain, and this little tale happened whilst at Leeds when we were playing Salford at The Willows in a Challenge Cup game.

Leeds were attacking in a hard-fought cup tie and there was nothing in it. We were battering on the home line when there was a collision between two Leeds players and both big Roy and our Aussie loose forward, Terry Webb, were laid out. Our physio signalled for a stretcher and the game was stopped and as there were no two-way radios in those days, I ran onto the field with the stretcher men to see the damage for myself.

Terry was concussed and was put onto the stretcher but thankfully big Roy stood up, shook his head and said, 'I'm OK Maurice, just give me a minute to come round,' and I helped him to the touchline.

I walked him to the half-way line and he seemed to be sound. 'Do you know where you are, Roy?' I asked.

'At Salford, in the cup tie,' he replied.

'What line is this?' I asked, pointing to the Salford 25 line as I walked Roy down the pitch again, all the time I could feel the big lad getting stronger.

'It's their 25' Roy said and I knew he was clear in his mind, but I'll just make sure I thought, so I walked him a bit further until we were at the Salford try line.

'And what line is this, Roy?' I asked.

Roy looked closely at the try line and said, 'Sorry, I don't know Maurice, I've never been as close to this line in my whole career.'

I knew then for sure that the big lad was OK. We went on to win the game and big Roy had a blinder!

Roy had been retired as a player for a few years and Super League was in full swing when I met up with him. Roy told me that he had been 'captured' in a pub by a well-meaning spectator and subjected, all night to the same question that he answered time and time again, 'It was a better game in your day, wasn't it Roy?'

Finally Roy, easygoing though he is, could take no more, and proceeded to explain once and for all the facts of rugby league life. 'When I was seventeen I was training one Tuesday night when our coach, Roy Francis, called me over and said "Get tomorrow off work because you are making your debut in the rearranged match up at Workington and we set off at 11am." I took the day off and it cost me a day's pay, travelled all that bloody way up there and in the first scrum, Bill Martin stuck the nut on me and broke my nose. It rained all through the bloody game, we got wet through and lost 38 points to 6 which meant losing pay of £8 less tax and National Insurance.

'On our way home Syd Hynes stopped the bus in Cockermouth as he knew the landlord of a pub and we got involved in a lock-in and got back on the bus at 2am and I had to be at work for 7:30am and to cap it all I had been drinking with two players who could shift a drop so my £8 less tax was gone double quick.

'I walked in home just in time for my mam to thrust some sandwiches in my hand and tell me that I had two minutes to catch my bus to work or I would be late. It was still pouring with rain, the damned bus was late and I stood there with water dripping off the plaster on my broken nose, expecting the sack or the biggest rollocking of my life from the boss for "knocking" yesterday, no sleep for 24 hours, skint because of the bloody £8 less tax and no pay for having the day off and because of getting stuffed at Workington, not knowing if I would ever get in the first team again, and you say it was a better game in my day! You must be bloody crackers' said Roy.

I think the spectator should have re-phrased his question to, 'They don't know they are born these days Roy'. He would have been nearer the mark.

If anyone ever gets the chance to see big Roy do his 'Tommy Cooper' thing, don't miss it, it's hilarious, as was his treatment of a bully at Lilleshall Sports centre when Roy quietened him wearing a red tennis ball like a clown's nose and asking the bully , 'Are you looking at my nose? I can't help my nose looking like a tennis ball. Now beat it before I lose my temper because of you staring at my nose.' The bully moved away very quickly indeed.

The one, the only, big Roy Dickinson.

KEN GEE

I am sure there are many who remember the late, great Wigan prop, Ken Gee. With the old leather scrum cap and the toe-end goal kicking style, Ken was a well-known figure on every ground in the years immediately after the Second World War and was one of many tremendously strong men who wore the Number 8 jersey at that time. The names trip off the tongue: Gee, Curran, Whitcombe, Prosser, Featherstone, Gwyther, Naughton and more.

Short in height by today's standards Ken was tremendously broad in the shoulders and chest with huge, strong arms and his power and scrum technique were legendary.

In 1946 the touring Lions had to take the only ship available to get them across the still dangerous waters to Australia and that was the aircraft carrier, *HMS Indomitable*.

Training during the six-week trip was conducted on the flight deck which had adequate space so long as the aircraft were not landing or taking off.

Unable to sail into Sydney because of The Great Australian Bight being still mined to stop invasion by Japan in the recent conflict, the tourists disembarked at Fremantle and then had to face a four-day, one track, train journey across the bottom of the continent to the Eastern seaboard to Sydney. There were no corridors on the train, no toilets and no water, except every two or three hundred miles at the few small stations dotted on the map. Players changed carriages at these stops to change their conversations with different players and it was at the final station that Ken and his best mate, another Wigan legend, Joe Egan, were joined by a nice young lady who had entered the train at Fremantle.

Now Ken was always a father figure, in fact he had a daughter almost as old as the young lady, and when, soon after setting off on the final lap to Sydney, the young girl started to sob and cry, Joe whispered to Ken, 'Find out what's wrong with this young girl.'

Ken leaned across the narrow compartment and in a soft, friendly, fatherly voice asked, 'What on earth is wrong, love?' the Lancashire brogue having a soothing effect on the girl who ceased sobbing.

'I'm in real trouble,' she confided to Ken, 'I'm pregnant'.

Ken was taken aback, as one would expect in 1946, but he tried to be positive about it and after a brief pause he said, 'Well I'm sure everything will turn out right love, anyway, it's not too bad these days, is it?'

The girl looked shocked, 'Oh it is,' she sobbed again.

'Why is it love?' Ken asked.

She answered, 'Because I wasn't pregnant when I got on this bloody train'.

As the Wigan coach I was having an after match pint with Joe Egan in the old Riverside Bar in the Central Park ground one winters afternoon when in came Ken Gee walking with the aid of two sticks. Joe told me that Ken was due to go into hospital next day for a hip replacement and was not looking forward to it at all. Joe had a seat ready for his old mate and Ken sat down with a bump, glad to take the weight off the injured hip.

'I've been thinking about how many of our old team have passed away recently and I blame Jim Sullivan,' Ken said to Joe.

Now the famous Wigan full-back, Jim Sullivan, had been the coach for years at Wigan and both Ken and Joe had played for him. 'Nay Ken, why blame poor old Jim, he's been passed away some years now,' said Joe.

'Yes, and I think he's up there,' Ken said, pointing a huge finger, heaven-wards, 'picking a team and he's already picked all our old mates who have passed on, and I go in for this operation tomorrow. I hope old Jim is not short of an open side prop when I'm under the knife!'

Ken made two tours in 1946 and 1950 along with his old mate, Joe Egan. It shows the prowess of Ken that in the nine tests played on those two tours, he played at number 8 in all nine games. He had a total of 17 international caps, every one gained by playing against the Aussies (9 times) and the

Kiwis (8 times) and on top of winning almost every medal in the book and being a cornerstone of that superb Wigan side of the late 1940s and early 1950s, Ken Gee was some man and some player.

JEFF GRAYSHON

Jeff was a tall, slim soccer player when he signed for Dewsbury and played his first professional rugby league at full-back at the old Crown Flatts ground.

Moved into the pack, he formed a very mobile second row partnership with a player who went on to be a Lions tourist himself, in 1974, John Bates.

In 1973 the Dewsbury team, coached by ex Wigan, Barrow and Featherstone loose forward, Tommy Smales, won the old Premiership 'top 8' cup beating Leeds at Odsal and Jeff was a key man in that success. The list of clubs he played for is both varied and impressive. Dewsbury, Bradford Northern, Leeds, Featherstone Rovers and Batley, plus a spell for Canterbury Bankstown in Sydney and of course, Yorkshire and Great Britain.

The last but one of his 13 caps for Great Britain was a unique occurrence as it made Jeff the oldest player ever to represent the country at 38 years when I brought him back to produce a story-book display in a crushing victory over New Zealand in the series second test at Wigan in 1985, in the game in which Gary Schofield scored four tries.

In the final test at Elland Road, the one in which Lee Crooks kicked the superb long-range penalty goal in injury time to draw the series, Jeff shared a record, on the day, with Shaun Edwards as the two became the oldest and the youngest players to play in a test match for Great Britain. Shaun lost that record to Paul Newlove some time later.

Jeff, despite receiving a serious leg injury playing in Australia, toured on the 1979 trip and played in five of the six tests against the Aussies and the Kiwis. I know one of his biggest disappointments was never playing in the Challenge Cup Final and he joined a most unlucky set of very good players who missed out on the big one in their careers.

Jeff also holds a special memory, actually held by one or two players, in that he played in the same team as his son, Paul, in professional rugby, and in fact Jeff can go one better, as he also played against his son, and I mean directly against his son, as both men were at number 8 that day. The tale goes thus.

Jeff had gone from Leeds to Featherstone to join his old friend and mentor, Peter Fox. Paul Grayshon had progressed his career at Odsal and had gained a first team place at open side prop. It had to happen that Bradford Northern were drawn to play at Featherstone's Post Office Road ground in the cup and Jeff was feeling chuffed at the prospect of facing his son, head on as it were, in the game. But not so Paul, who when he called in to see his mum in the week before the game, hardly spoke to Jeff, and he had kept out of his dad's way all that week.

Came the match day and as Jeff ran out with his team, the Bradford lads were out already, so being right with his son, Jeff ran over to Paul and shook hands. As they were parting, Paul said, 'You can have it hard or easy today, it's up to you,' leaving Jeff in no doubt about his sons intentions towards him!

Now Jeff had mixed it with the best but this was their 'young 'un' and he felt a bit uneasy that Paul should take it so seriously. Anyway, Bradford kicked off to Featherstone and it was a high kick that flew straight to Jeff who was stood about five yards infield from the touchline. Jeff caught it and just got his pass inside as Paul arrived and hit Jeff, fair and square with his shoulder and sent his dad, at a good rate of knots, on the seat of his pants, CRASH, into the advertising boards around the perimeter of the pitch.

An old retired coal miner was leaning on the rail right above where Jeff's progress was halted by the boards, complete with flat cap and miner's muffler. With that typical dry pit-top humour, the elder statesman supporter said, 'If I were thee Jeff, I'd smack his arse and send him to bed!'

All big Jeff could do was smile.

A smashing bloke is Jeff Grayshon and I will always remember the phone call I made to him after I had racked my brain to find a prop good enough for that second Kiwi test, 'Will you do a job for me against the Kiwis, Jeff?' and without hesitation he said, 'I will that Maurice, and don't worry old mate, we will do 'em.' and we did, Jeff.

I had brought Jeff back to play in the President's Cup game against France in Limoux in the June prior to the Kiwi tests and we won despite a big fight in which the diminutive French wingman snuck up behind Jeff and hit him a beauty that cut the big man's eye. Most of the fights stopped and the players rolled about laughing at the sight of Jeff chasing the small, very quick wingman, with no chance of catching him. He tried though and it's a good job he didn't.

KEITH MASON Snr

Keith was a tough front rower who loved to be in the thick of the action. 6'3", 17 stone plus, he was, as they say these days, a big unit. He could also street fight with the best, as he proved once in a confrontation with a man as big as himself on the old Crown Flatt ground, Dewsbury, when he defended one of his team mates who was being outmatched in a punch-up.

Big Mason destroyed the aggressor in a few seconds with a show of speed, power and ferocity rarely seen these days.

Keith also took some stick too, as in a well-remembered

tussle with the redoubtable Aussie test hard man, Les Boyd, but he tells a story that epitomises those tough days when he relates his battle at the Craven Cottage ground of the Fulham club in their opening season of 1980.

That super half-back, Reg Bowden was the club's first player-coach and he assembled a huge pack and a hard all-round side which achieved promotion in their first season. Keith went to London with a Dewsbury team that were on the small side and he saw his job as that of 'protector of the innocents'.

'Harry' Beverley was opposite Keith in the scrum and the pair battled all afternoon as props did then. Beverley was a big, tough lad himself and had an unusual running style in that be brought his knees up high and was an awkward man to tackle.

In the scoring stakes Keith must have been about six to five in front as big Harry levelled it up when he flattened Keith with those big knees on his way to scoring a try and Keith required treatment and was being revived by the magic sponge as Harry was walking back from scoring.

With Keith on his knees and Harry being in the vicinity the big Fulham prop decided to go one up and simply kicked Keith as he was passing. 'One up to me Mason' said Harry as Keith then needed further treatment for the kick. Harry Beverley must have respected Keith for him to speak at all, as Harry was a man of few words! Mutual respect, I can assure you.

The softer hearted side of Keith Mason is seen in a tale he tells when, after having a good season for Dewsbury, he was sought after by David Ward, the then Hunslet coach, along with Peter Jarvis.

Wardy found out where Keith lived and went to the big man's house to discuss his personal terms. The only thing was that no one had mentioned it to Keith and the sight of the no-nonsense David Ward marching up Keith's garden path was too much for the big prop, and, calling to his wife, 'It's Wardy, I bet he's coming to sign me, tell him I'm out'.

Keith dived under the table and pulled the cover down to hide himself. 'Come in, David.' Keith's missus said, 'He's in, he's just under the table!'

Now that is straight John Bull true. Keith signed for Wardy and had a real time playing at the superb Elland Road ground.

On one occasion taking his wife down to the railway station, as she was going to London to visit family, Keith acted the doting husband and carried her case into the carriage and was chatting away to her when he suddenly felt the train lurch forward on its way to The Smoke with the big man still aboard.

The train was away like Martin Offiah giving Keith no chance of jumping off, so it was a nice little run across to Doncaster before he could get out. A phone call to his mate to come and collect him was made because, you guessed it, he had no money on him as he had taken an hour off work to see their lass off!

It could only happen to a prop.

Keith was lumbered, as a young man, with a nickname that dishonoured him, and no one ever dared use it to his face. When playing for Wakefield Wildcats his son Keith Jr was on TV and a well-known commentator, at the moment of young Mason making a mistake said, 'Oh dear, young ******', just like his dad'. The dreaded nickname was used and the fearsome dad heard it on the box, in front of millions of viewers.

Some time later, the commentator was visiting his mum in

Dewsbury and Keith knew this and that evening went to a well-known pub in the town centre which the commentator used when in the area, to sort him out. The man even phoned me to get me to speak to Keith in an attempt to smooth it out, but Keith was hurt by the remark, which no doubt was just a throwaway line not intended to be smart, but nevertheless said.

In time the hurt healed but the commentator kept well out of the big man's way until it was safe to come out! Keith Mason has a soft spot bigger than himself, a cracking kid.

ANONYMOUS

Another true tale about a good prop forward or hooker, again from that hot-bed birthplace of talented footballers, Hunslet and a tale that shows again how much the times have changed.

I was at Halifax as coach, with my old pal, Ronnie Dobson, as football director. We wanted a young forward who had been staying away from his club because of a financial disagreement and managed to get the lad on a month's loan, with a view to sign him if all was in place at the month's end.

When the loan period was up Ronnie and I arranged to call at the player's home to talk about how much money he would be looking for to join us at Thrum Hall. We were a bit early as the player was working over and hadn't arrived home yet so his dad made us a cuppa and we were having a chat.

The dad was delighted we were interested in his son and explained to us how we had changed him since he had been with us this last month. 'He has altered overnight. He was out boozing every night before you came for him, now he hardly goes out. Mondays he nips down to the local to pay his Wembley money and Tuesday nights he trains with you and has a couple on his way home. Wednesday he takes his bird out for a drink and Thursday he is with you again and calls in for the darts and dominoes at the local as he captains the team. Friday and Saturday he is out with the girlfriend, only a couple of hours each night and Sunday, after the game, he likes a few pints with the lads from Halifax. Apart from that he never goes out of the house.'

His dad meant well but the player wanted more money than we could afford and unfortunately we parted company. It's a good job too otherwise Ronnie and I may have had to call in AA.

TERRY DEWHIRST

They say that people only talk about you if you are a 'good 'un'. Well, if that's the case, Terry Dewhirst must be a world beater! I don't know of a man with as many tales surrounding him as Terry. One of the first things that strikes you is that when in conversation about the man, one never calls him Terry, he is always given the respected title of TD.

A Batley lad, and one who always calls Batley, 'Barfield', as a motion picture was shot in the town in the 1940s and instead of using the correct name of Batley, they called the town, Barfield, and amongst the locals, it stuck, Terry was educated at the small Catholic school of St Mary's and was raised amongst hard-working, hard-drinking staunch rugby league men.

Remembering that the background to the game in Terry's home town was deep set with traditional ways as the Batley club hold a wonderful record from those early days of our game when they won the proud, new Challenge Cup three times in the first five years of its existence, 1897, 1898 and 1901. And over 100 years later that record still holds dear to the folk of Batley and no one is as prouder of it than TD.

Everybody in 'Barfield' knows big Terry and they all engage him in conversation regarding the game and its general welfare. He has a retentive memory where the game is concerned and can fire off dates, venues, scores and scorers like we recite our two times tables.

In his time his jobs have been both interesting and varied: professional rugby league prop forward, a coal miner, welder, bookmaker and landlord, he was also a renowned street fighter in his youth, caused mainly from his inability to walk away should anyone have the bad judgement to offer him out!

A big, strong man, Terry's lumbering gait belied his nimbleness of foot and his victories are well noted in the Heavy Woollen area. He still does not suffer fools gladly, as one meeting with the local postman, who is certainly nobody's fool, shows.

The postman mentioned that he was a bit miffed with a cup final because of the closeness of the contest and he liked to see a clear winner. 'That's part of a good final when the result goes to the last few seconds of a game,' pointed out Terry but the postman stuck to his guns and Terry could not win the argument so his parting broadside was, 'Well you don't understand the game, so it's a waste of time trying to educate you'. The postman swore revenge for himself and this is where the Barfield humour comes to bear.

He wrote to the local weekly paper and submitted his best ever international team and included Lewis Jones, Alex Murphy, Brian Bevan, Lionel Cooper and Arthur Clues. Terry phoned me and told me about the conversation with the postman and about the team he had selected. 'What do you think his front row is?' Terry asked me, he continued, 'Gee, Egan and me.' said Terry. 'He's got his own back. I can just hear 'em all in the pub tonight, they will be saying "Dewhirst's not good enough to be in that team!"'

That's Barfield for you!

Cricket is another of Terry's loves and he always fancied himself as an opening batsman. We were involved at the Bramley club together and a benefit cricket match was arranged for one of the players who was celebrating ten years at the club.

The game was against a local league side and was played in a very friendly manner as Terry opened the innings, taking first strike. The bowler opening the attack for the league side was pretty quick and our hero never saw the ball as it smashed into his pads, as plumb out as one could be, 'Howzat!' yelled the bowler, stumper, slips, third man and five blokes passing on the number 27 bus.

Without hesitation the umpire, who did not know Terry, or of his passion for winning, raised the dreaded finger, 'Out, leg before,' he said.

Terry stood there like a bemused, stunned gargantuan. As the penny dropped that he was out, his anger rose, 'Tha' what?' he stormed, staring at the umpire, who, in the genteel sport of leather against willow had never seen an angry man so close, again Terry said, 'Tha' what, out? If tha' thinks I'm coming all 'tway from Barfield to be out first ball tha's wrong.'

The quiet living, placid umpire took one look at the threatening giant, with the cauliflower ear and broken nose and coughed politely saying, 'Not out, going down leg side. It would have missed leg stump.'

The bowler was beside himself but got Terry last ball of the over, knocking both middle and leg pegs out of the ground. The big man accepted his fate and walked.

As A team coach at Bramley, Terry played a few games for me, one in particular, at his home town ground of Mount Pleasant, Batley. On a cold, wind and rain-swept Saturday afternoon in mid-winter there was only one spectator in the whole of the ground and he had his young son with him to watch a match at the 'Mount' involving this passionate lone spectator's beloved Batley.

A scrum was ordered by the referee on the half-way line, five yards in from touch, as it was in those days, and the ball was a long way away so the scrum stood up, waiting for the ball to be returned when Terry, with nothing else to do, noticed the lone spectator sat in the stand only a few yards from him, and, of course, Terry knew him from school.

Now it must be remembered that Terry was a legend in Batley, well-respected and well thought of and there he was, wet through, caked in thick mud with water dripping off his nose, holding up a young whipper-snapper of a hooker, and worst still, playing in an A team game. Terry, poignantly, called up to the lone spectator, 'Hey up, Joe, do you remember me when I was a good 'un?'

The stories abound when Terry was a landlord. He had several pubs in Halifax, Dewsbury and Batley and, in the old tradition of good innkeepers, kept his pubs clean and his ale in good nick. He was in the old William Deighton pub in Halifax which, was next door to the YEB electrical showrooms, when they were demolishing the ancient buildings opposite.

It was summer time and the demolition men were ready for a pint or two of Terry's Tetley Bitter each evening when they had finished work. Now Terry had a good contact for some beautiful pork pies and he had decided to serve these pies warmed up and he'd seen one of these newfangled microwave ovens in the YEB, so he bought one. One of the demolition lads came in, black bright, but thirsty and enquired after the price of a warm pork pie. 'I'll have one.' the lad said and Terry, using the microwave for the first time, cut the pie in half and, leaving the all-steel knife on the plate, put the whole lot in the oven and switched it on.

At the bell Terry took out the plate and served the lad, stood at the bar. Suddenly there was a howl of pain as the lad picked up the knife which stuck to his hand and he started a strange dance around the bar, trying to shake off the knife that was causing so much agony. He finally removed the knife and went to the hospital.

That evening we had trained at Thrum Hall and a few of us went down to Terry's for a drink. As we went in there was the lad, all cleaned up and with a huge bandage around his hand which was in a sling. 'How's the bitter tonight?' asked one of our players.

'The bitter's sound,' said the injured demolition man, 'but take my advice, don't get a bloody warm pie!' he moaned. He was excellent at learning through other people's mistakes was Terry.

Another pub TD took was the Victoria on Bradford Road, Batley. A smaller pub than the William Deighton, it suited Terry as it was in his territory and again he kept everything just right. He had been in the place a few years and had the chance of taking another pub with more food potential (not pork pies), so he was marking time waiting to move out when a mate of mine, who worked in the building trade, was rained off one morning and called in to see Terry just as he opened up at 11:30am.

A regular customer arrived at the same time as my mate, and this customer too was an elderly bricklayer and was rained off as well. Terry served both men and then produced a piece of paper and a pencil stub and started, painstakingly, to write out a list. The bricky ordered another pint and as Terry was pulling it the bricky, just trying to be sociable, said, 'Are you writing a bet out Terry?'

It was obvious that Terry was in bad humour and wanted

a bit of quiet whilst he completed his list. 'No,' he snapped, 'I am coming out of here soon and I'm making a list for when I'm out.'

The elderly bricklayer didn't take the hint and said, 'Is it a list for leaving presents?'

'You could say that, but it's a list of everyone who has taken the micky out of me when I was this side of the bar and they were on your side of the bar, I'm going to give them a present all right.' said Terry, clenching a huge fist in front of the bricky.

'Am I on the list?' the old tradesman said nervously.

Terry finished pulling the pint, placed it carefully before the bricky and said, with a sickly smile, 'You'll have to wait and see, won't you'. Just like the Godfather!

Terry Dewhirst had started his playing career at school where the sports master was Mr Derek Brown, a first class referee who had been in charge of all the top matches in the rugby league calendar at some time or other. Now Mr Brown was still a first team referee when Terry had signed as a professional for Halifax and was in charge of a third round Challenge Cup game at Thrum Hall, in which Warrington, led by the redoubtable Alex Murphy, were the visitors.

It was a no-nonsense, old-fashioned, no holds barred cup tie with personal vendettas going on all over the field. Alex was a master of the skill of drawing players into the game he wanted them to play and he did this excellently this day at Halifax, gaining crucial penalties for the Wire and causing frustration amongst some Halifax players, TD being one. Terry blew his top with Alex and threw a haymaker at the clever half-back, which missed by a country mile. Alex dropped as if pole-axed and Mr Brown frustrated Terry even further when he pointed dramatically to the dressing room and uttered the chilling word, 'Off'.

Terry threw himself on Mr Brown's mercy, 'But Mr Brown, sir, you were my teacher.' Hoping that the fact would gain Terry a reprieve, but no, 'Off, I said.' the stern referee repeated and the despondent Halifax prop turned dejectedly away.

As Terry passed the prostrate Alex, the Warrington player/coach opened his eyes, and looking at Terry who he had contrived successfully to get sent off, winked cheekily at Terry as he passed him. A quick appealing last look at Mr Brown, who had missed the wink and was still pointing towards the dressing room, decided Terry's next move and he marched over to Alex, and kicked him on the ground! This action caused the whole Warrington team to run to the aid of their coach, whom Terry had missed again with the kick, and they formed two lines and as Terry walked between them, they, each one, took a swing at the big prop as he trudged off the pitch, with Alex, all the while, laughing to himself.

From school Terry went to the successful Mirfield Boys Club and from there to the terrific Dewsbury Celtic team. It was from the Celtic that he signed for Halifax and received a John Player Trophy winners' medal in the 1971–72 season. Terry concentrated on his pub for a few seasons then came back for the much respected Arthur Keegan at Bramley, then later still in 1978 for me at Halifax.

In the days that Terry went to play for Dewsbury Celtic, it was only one short step away from professional rugby, as the Leeds and District league was a very competitive one with lots of ex-professionals in it and each team had at least one or two amateur internationals playing for them.

Terry was just nineteen when one Thursday training night the then coach at the Celtic, who had played with the club for years and knew everything about the game called Terry over and said, 'We have a tough match against Bisons away on Saturday and I'm going to give you your debut. So don't be late for the bus and best of luck.'

At that time it was like playing for a professional side as the team was in the local newspaper each Friday morning, match reports were published from last week's game and it meant a lot to your mum and dad if you were in the Celtic team as it was a close knit society around the area of Westown, the Irish 'Nash' club and St Polinus Catholic Church.

An excited Terry Dewhirst was too early for the bus on the Saturday so, with a bit of time to kill, he called in the Nash for a lemonade. Carrying his boots, jock-strap, shoulder pads and an assortment of strapping that all props carried in those days in an Asda carrier bag, Terry bumped into an old school mate in the Nash who had been shopping that Saturday morning. After a long chin-wag, Terry said so-long to his mate, picked up his carrier bag and embarked on the team bus for Bisons.

On arrival the coach growled, 'Get ready' and Terry, nervous owing to the enormity of the game, was stripped to his underpants in record time and reached for his carrier bag in which resided his playing gear. Imagine his horror when on opening the plastic bag he found his mate's T-bone steak, sausage, tomatoes, mushrooms and a bag of spuds. He had picked up his mate's carrier and had to suffer the wrath of the fierce Celtic coach's tongue. But spare a thought for Terry's mate, who, expecting a slap-up meal found only Terry's size 12s and a jock strap. Terry borrowed some boots and had a blinder.

A legend in his own life time, TD.

ANONYMOUS

My contract as Great Britain coach took in the selection, preparation and coaching of the Under-21 sides. On our first trip together, to the delightful town of Albi in the Tarn department of Southern France, to take on the French Under-24s, I selected a strong, talented group of players, all of whom would go on to full international level. The side was skippered by Lee Crooks (Hull) already a full cap player and included a pack containing Paul Groves (Salford), Shaun Wayne (Wigan), Andy Dannett (Hull), Paul Round (Saints), Gary Divorty (Hull) and Mike Gregory (Warrington).

Deryck Fox was at scrum-half to fetch and carry for this impressive pack. The game was won and we returned to the team hotel for our after-match meal and then out for a quiet drink.

At that time the forerunner of today's academy set up was the 'colts', the Under-18s, who regularly played the French Under-21s in international fixtures and they were coached by the excellent former Wigan forward, the late Geoff Lyon. Geoff was helping me in Albi and we set off together for a nice gentle night out in this beautiful little town.

On arrival back at the hotel we found that the complete squad were up in arms as three of our group had crossed swords with a Catalan mob and had come off the worse for wear, nothing more serious than dented pride. Geoff and I sorted the team out and retired them to bed and I checked with the night staff that the foyer was the only exit and Geoff and I lounged there all night, just in case the troops marched again.

By all accounts two players, a back and a forward, had 'clicked' with two French girls who knew about this club that opened all night. Our two boys paid at the door for all four, then the two girls disappeared inside and the four bouncers, Catalan heavies, then refused the lads entry, and gave our boys a good hiding when they demanded their money back.

On their way back to the hotel they came across another of our forwards, a big, tough kid who saw the condition of his two mates and forced them to take him to these hard men and he would get their money back! Our hero was eating a hot dog as they approached the night club and after threatening all four bouncers with terrible vengeance, they picked him up and threw him through a shop window. Our man was so tough (or drunk) that as he was sat in the window bottom he was still clutching the hot dog!

His two mates retrieved him from the window and all three went back to the hotel for reinforcements, that's when Geoff and I stopped the battle of Albi.

Needless to say the press who were on the trip blew the incident up out of all proportion, typical! But truth will out!

8

HOOKERS

PETER CLARKE

In the days of competitive scrimmaging, the hooker was wide open to physical assault before, during and after a scrum.

Before a scrum, just as the two packs of forwards' heads touched was a vulnerable time for the number nine as many a punch was loosened at the hooker and many an elbow was aimed at the ball-getter at that time.

During a scrum was a dangerous time too as both packs tussled with each other in an effort to gain advantage, one over the other, it was the time that an experienced second rower would try out his Sunday punch on an unsuspecting hookers nose or jaw.

After the scrum was the favourite time for the old head as he would wait around three seconds, then smack the hooker in the kisser, just as he thought the danger had passed and was relaxing!

The scrums became more civilised with the advent of head, ball and possession at the scrum. No pushing and wheeling, no challenging for the strike on entry, just steady away – you get the head, you get the feed and you get the ball – as simple as that.

All the hookers today look like Tom Cruise or Brad Pitt, when, in the olden days, most looked like Rocky Marciano or Mike Tyson.

I was once out and about with Peter Clarke and we met up, right out of the blue with a former international hooker who had crossed swords with Peter on many occasions and when Peter went for another cup of tea the other hooker said, 'When Peter walked over to me I didn't know whether to shake his hand or duck for cover!'

A hard breed all right, and clever technicians, those men who held a repertoire of highly secret tricks of how to position their body to win the ball in the tight scrum, this altering against every hooker they played against as what may work against one, may not work against another. They would look for, then lock away in their memory, any habit or idiosyncrasy that an opposing scrum-half may have, and work out little ciphers with their own half-back on how the ball would be put into the set scrum, to spin it in, with the bias of the spin aimed at breaking the ball back towards your own hooker as it touched the ground, or not to spin it but throw it hard up into your opposing hooker's face – until this was outlawed later!

Against the head the hooker was a long way from the ball and nine times out of ten his 'strike' path was obstructed by the legs of the opposite hooker, so he would slyly watch for the scrum-half's stockings to appear at the tunnel of the scrum and either time his strike to beat his opposite man, or, block the other hooker's legs with his own and let his open side prop win the ball. A million tricks as I said, all aimed at one end product, possession of the football!

Like all good hookers, Peter Clarke hated losing a scrum. He would come up with the strangest reasons should he lose one. I have heard him complain that 'The referee got in the way' or 'The sun was in my eyes' or 'That little b****** (the other scrum half) is putting it in his second row.' But should he lose a scrum then Peter would somehow drop onto the ground in the middle of the pack and scrabble on all fours after the disappearing pill to try to retrieve it by hand! He just would not accept losing that ball.

I said before that Peter was the best ball winner I ever coached and I had some great ball winners: David Ward, Colin Falcon, David Watkinson, Russ Bridge, Paul O'Hara, Dean Raistrick, Gary Brentley, Dean Blankley, Glynn Lewis, Nicky Kiss, Ray Tabern, Neil Kelly and Derek Wroe to name but a few, but Clarkey was the tops in winning that precious pill.

One of several brothers who all played professional rugby, Peter was playing amateur rugby and had gained selection for the Lancashire County side to play in the Inter-County Championships when his oldest brother, the late Geoff, who was now a rugby league referee of some note, told Peter that the Rochdale Hornets chairman had expressed an interest in him when Geoff had officiated at Rochdale only that weekend.

Peter decided to get his Lancashire cap then have a go at the professional game and Geoff pulled out his fixture card and said, 'Lancashire play in two weeks' time and I've got Rochdale A in a month, so I'll tell the chairman that you will play in that game and I'll give you a fair crack our kid'. Now that sounded like a good deal to Peter, so he agreed.

Come the day and Clarkey was excited at the prospect of turning pro, as he ran out on the old Recreation Ground at the Hornets, to play Swinton A on that wintry afternoon, but their kid was refereeing and he had promised Peter a fair go. First scrum Geoff blew his whistle, 'Feet across Rochdale hooker, penalty kick,' and so it went on, scrum after scrum. Geoff did Peter for loose arm, feet across, handing out, swearing and every foul in the book. The culmination was in the final minutes of the match, with the score at six all, a scrum was formed only five yards from the Swinton line and, although against the head, Peter used all his skill and timing as he struck like a cobra, hooked the ball behind his heels and watched his half-back pick up the ball to dive over the

Swinton try line for the winner, just as the scrum collapsed.

It was then that Peter heard the dreaded whistle and his brother's voice call out in a commanding tone, 'Feet across again Rochdale, come here Hornets number nine'.

Peter was incensed; their kid had promised him a fair crack and yet had crucified him all afternoon. His blood boiled at the thought of Geoff doing him out of his moment of glory and temper raged through him as he pulled himself from the wreckage of that final scrum and ran, yes, ran to his brother who had played the dirtiest of tricks on him. Stopping only inches from Geoff's face, through the tears of absolute frustration Peter yelled, 'Wait until we get home, I'm going to tell my dad about you!'

This was the hard case hooker, Peter Clarke, who once told me that when he had Alan Hodgkinson and Peter Birchall, years later at the Hornets as his props, he was the biggest bully in the league.

Young Clarkey signed for Rochdale and gave many years of great service to the club before 'doing the rounds' in the league.

In his latter years I was lucky enough to sign Peter three times, at Huddersfield, Wigan and Bramley and good times were had at all three clubs. At Bramley I managed to get together a very good pack of forwards with a cracking back three of Karl Harrison, Alan Clarkson and Ken Loxton. The front row was second to none in the division with Alan Hindley, Tony Garforth and big George Ballentyne as the props and that man Clarkey at number nine.

George was on loan to us from Castleford and the bearded giant, with terrific pace for a nineteen stoner, gave us that defence-bursting power runner to go with the fleet footed Harrison and Clarkson. The scene is set for a Good Friday evening game at Lawkholme Lane, Keighley. We had trained on Thursday at Bramley and big George had complained of having the 'runs' all day, 'something I must have eaten' he said. On arriving home on Thursday evening after training, and arranging to go to Keighley under our own steam, without the cost of a bus, George phoned me in a state of anxiety saying that the runs had worsened and that he could keep nothing in himself!

I advised him strongly to attend his doctor's surgery on Good Friday morning and let me know during the day of his progress. George was a crucial member of the pack and I wanted him in against Keighley as we had an outside chance of promotion.

The big forward reported three times during Friday saying that he had stopped 'running' and, although feeling a bit wheezy, would give it a go at Lawkholme.

Everyone arrived at Keighley on time but George looked white and drawn. 'I'll be OK' he said and changed into his playing kit. Mr Peter Massey from Manchester, was the referee, and as he checked the studs and shoulder pads he said to me, 'Big George looks a bit strange,' and I explained his situation to Mr Massey.

We kicked off on a beautiful warm, still spring evening and the first scrum was about ten minutes into the game. George mustered his front row together, Harrison and Clarkson slammed into the second row, right in behind big George. When the weight of the Keighley pack came forward onto George, he was caught in a vice-like situation and the inevitable happened. Harrison and Clarkson have never moved so quickly, and Ken Loxton, never renowned as a speed merchant, was away like a rat up a pipe. So too Tony Garforth on the blind side, only Clarkey remained at his post, at a reasonable distance away of course, to see if George required any assistance, but George was rooted to the spot, afraid to move a muscle until he was helped to the dressing

'I'm handing you the ball Maurice because you dropped the last five passes.' The author (left) at a dinner at Eccles Amateur Rugby League Club, Manchester.

Geoff Fletcher passing the ball. This is a collector's item as there is a suggestion of a bit of hair on Geoff's head!

This tackler of the great John Holmes must be the Rugby Football League's official deodorant sniffer.

The fabulous 'Mick Sully' Michael Sullivan.

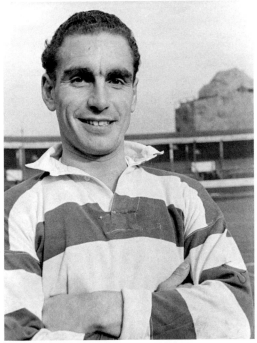

The 'Lion King' himself, peerless Stan McCormick, without his horses head cane!

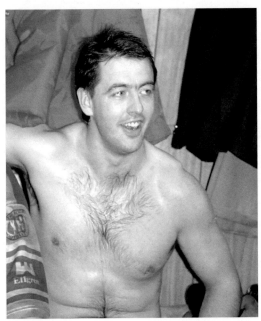

I always told Joe Lydon not to back the horses as he would lose his shirt one day!

*Dicky Williams, a little red-haired football genius
and one of my schoolboy heroes.*

*One of the most underrated footballers of his day, Kenny Loxton, obviously about to sell a
dummy!*

The 'father figure' on the train from Fremantle to Sydney, the great Ken Gee.

Big Jeff Grayshon, a cracking prop who came to realise early in a game that his son had grown up.

Widnes' Mick Adams must have thought he had run into a brick wall when Steve Pitchford tackled him, with David Ward in close attendance.

Tough Frank Birkin leads an equally tough Albert Fearnley, who is thinking, 'So that's where my spare scrum-cap went.'

The holder of the longest recorded goal kick in rugby league history, the great Cumbrian, Martin Hodgson.

My all-time favourite hero, the big man himself, Arthur Clues, the ex-copper who came over from Sydney for three years and stayed for life – the best all-round forward I ever saw!

If there were three tougher then they must have been supermen! Derek Turner, John 'Joby' Shaw and Jack Wilkinson.

Wigan's champion Andy Farrell on the charge with Warrington's Briers no doubt thinking, 'Jesus, what am I doing here?'

The 'catch as catch can' wrestling champion, star Huddersfield forward and member of the famous Rorkes Drift Tour, Dougie Clark.

To this day, still spoken of with great respect, the superb Great Britain, England, Yorkshire, Batley, Dewsbury and Leeds loose forward, Frank Gallagher.

The classic ball handler and copybook tackler, Ken Traill.

The Aussies named him 'The Wild Bull of the Pampas' but most players called him Sir! The terrific Vinty Karalius.

The super little Manchester referee, Peter Massey, tells the wonderful Wally Lewis, 'That way to the airport Wally, off you go.'

The current Saints kicking tee carrier and baggage man Stan Wall tells Jeff Grayshon, 'I'm getting neck ache talking to you Jeff, so keep your team in order.'

'I'm telling thee so you had better listen fellas.' Peter Fox lays down the law.

Jimmy Hornby says, 'I grew this tash to be like Maurice because everyone says I am Bamford's eldest lad!'

The man who fostered Australian rugby league and to whom the much respected 'Dally M' medal is named after, the superb Dally Messenger.

Another wonderful Aussie wing man, the hugely powerful Lionel Cooper of Huddersfield.

'How on earth could he play?' they asked, but boy, could he! The one and only Brian 'The Great Bev' Bevan, another fabulous Australian.

In his day the finest stand off, from New Zealand, Ces Mountford, a wonderful player and coach.

Another all-time great but this time from South Africa who arrived a Springbok and went home a legend, top wing man, Tom Van Vollenhoven.

Nothing can be said about this man's bravery that would do justice to how brave he really is. My old Great Britain under 21s player who went on to skipper his country in full internationals and become a super coach, dear Mike Gregory.

The original beast himself who put the bejasus up the Aussies in their own backyard. Kevin Ward was a powerful front rower whose career was cut short because of injury, but what a prop he was, easily the best in his day.

Dai Watkins, David to us poor English. A dual international and brilliant record-breaking goal kicker who coached Great Britain as well. A wonderful crowd pleaser and a great ambassador for both codes.

room to be literally hosed down with the hose pipe in the changing area, never to return that night. The area of the scrum was swilled down with water and the game continued!

Peter Clarke's final game as a professional player was for Bramley in the game that the great Ken Loxton suffered that unfortunate injury that ended his career. It was at Ninian Park, Cardiff. On the trip down to the principality Peter told me that this would be his last game, it was the last game of the season so he hadn't left us in a spot, but I knew that it was not only the end of his career but the end of an era as Peter was the last of the original breed of hooker.

All the game Peter was having a running battle with that grand forward of both codes, Tommy David. Peter was on top first, then Tommy and tempers were fraying when Tommy was injured in the collision with Ken Loxton and both players left the field.

The hooter went to end the game and I went on to Peter to thank him for his contribution to all the three clubs we had worked at together and we were walking off the pitch when Tommy David arrived to confront Peter and say, 'You dirty bugger, Clarkey. I'm going to give you a choice; you can have it twice next season or now, at the back of the stand'.

Peter thought for a moment and said, 'Can I have it next season Tommy?'

Tommy David said 'And you will get it too'.

Peter stood back a bit and smiling said, 'I won't Tommy because I've just retired,' and walked straight passed the bemused Tommy David into the dressing rooms.

Held in high esteem is my old mate Peter Clarke.

PHIL MARTIN

When I went to Halifax as coach in 1987, players with professional experience were thin on the ground there.

Having one or two mates in the coaching game, I did the rounds to see if there were any players at pro clubs that would come to Thrum Hall for first team football as opposed to staying in the A team where they were. Paul Daly was at Hunslet and told me I could have Phil on a free transfer.

I had known Phil from his Castleford Lock Lane days and, whilst not being the best ball winner in the league, he was certainly better than most on the books at the time, so we signed him. Now Phil was one mickey taker, and his slow, easy way often misled people into thinking he was a soft touch; my word how wrong they were. He was one tough cookie, but with that wicked mining area sense of humour and fun and he fit perfectly into what I was looking for at the time.

Phil told me of a low time in his life when he was going through the trauma of the death of his mum. Being the eldest son, the job of distributing the good lady's ashes was given to Phil by his siblings and, obviously thinking the world of his mum, he agreed to do so.

Now it was just before Christmas that Phil rounded up his three best mates, all professional rugby players and all could shift a 'drop' or two. Phil needed his mates for moral support and he hand picked them as all three had the fondest memories of Phil's mum who was a very respected lady.

They decided that a drop of Dutch courage was required, so calling in the local, and having topped up with Tetley Bitter, the intrepid foursome set off, in the quickly oncoming dark of that winter's afternoon, to the cemetery to place the good lady's remains with those of her late husband on the family plot.

The cemetery was by the side of the fast-flowing, coal-black river in the Aire Valley and Phil, carrying his beloved mum under his arm, like Ernest Ward walking out at Wembley in 1947, strode manfully with his mates towards the final resting place. Now Phil would be the first to admit that he did not possess the safest hands in the game and whilst he was a good dummy half, he was not at his best on a rainy, dark, afternoon with a belly full of Tetley's. He half slipped on the river bank and 'Plop' into the river went his late mum.

Only a superhuman effort, with a four man sprint downstream on the bank and a human chain of linked bodies across the foaming, wild racing river saved the bobbing, fast-moving cherished urn. It was retrieved and the task of love completed by four very wet, very drunk professional rugby league players, who were proud to be involved in that final service for a well loved and respected lady.

It was Phil too that as a young single lad about town, was found by a certain young woman's husband in a very compromising situation with his wife. Instead of the good hiding Phil expected, the husband took Phil into the kitchen and said, 'What do you want, tea or coffee?'

What a man, Phil Martin.

9

SHORT UNION TALES, NICKNAMES AND NORTHERN TRAITS

ANONYMOUS

No matter what any rugby league man thinks of the rugby union game there is no getting away from the fact that if the Twickenham traditionalists had not been so bloody minded and stupid way back in 1895, then there would be no rugby league today. No doubt the fifteen a side game could have been made of sterner stuff prior to open professionalism being installed a few short years ago, if the break away had not taken place, but the toughness of today's top union players can not be challenged now that the game has become a job of work and not a 'money in your boot after the match' shamateurism.

Out in the open it's a competitive, tough game, with the forward handling skills and the three-quarter defensive attitudes improved out of all proportion. But like all sports that evolve into full professionalism, something very important is always lost.

The old amateur way, with its playing for the involvement of the game alone for the game's sake, had a nice traditional feel, like when we were kids playing at school or in amateur football when we had to pay our subs to play. In those days fly-halves (stand-offs) and scrum-halves were not supposed to get involved in tackling, that was the forwards' job, the donkeys they were called, but the class-conscious game even differentiated amongst forwards.

For instance second rowers were line-out jumpers, the number 8 was the thinker in the pack and the wing forwards did have a defensive role, usually to knock the fly-half down from the scrum and kill any loose balls at the rucks and mauls, that left the tackling onus on the props and hooker, whose specialist jobs were in scrimmaging only.

So there was a class level throughout the game, but not so much in the cold North as in the opulent Midlands and South. Hence onto a little tale about a Southern gentleman, whose job, in a national bank, brought him up to the Borough of Morley.

He was from the Harlequins club and he was a traditional number 8. Because of his club pedigree, the selection committee selected him but his North Country team mates found him a bit short in the ticker department and lazy to boot. The Morley club at the time was a graveyard for all the fancy sides as they were a working class, no-nonsense, hard-nut team that took no prisoners and expected every man to stand his corner.

In the dressing room before his second appearance, the Morley captain, a respected, hard-nosed back rower who was a good county class forward, looked straight into the eyes of the ex-Harlequins player and said, 'I would like you to jump at four o'clock today, then again at ten past'.

He had made his point. A quick word with his manager and he was back in Harlequins thirds the following week!

ALAN COXAN

The rumour that all props are a bit dim is not true, or so I'm told. Alan Coxan was a big prop from the Durham area who came to play a game at Morley with Durham and didn't go back home for many years.

As a Tetley's rep, Alan learned the pub trade and a few years later was ready to open his own bar in Morley. Everything was in place except the name for the new bar and try as he might Alan could not come up with a catchy name that would take on with the kids and the quiet drinkers to ensure a good cross-clientele. Alan went training this night and, calling in at the clubhouse for a pint, he noticed a double table completely surrounded by props, as they called such a meeting in Morley, a 'thicket of front rowers!' Alan was at his wits end so he asked the props to think of a name for his new bar, something trendy, with a zing to it. An hour later Alan was going home and as he passed the props he asked, 'How about it, any luck?'

The leader of the props said, 'after great deliberation we can only come up with "Coxan's"'. I rest my case!

ANONYMOUS

A classic tale is the story of the young prop from the Burley RUFC who received his cash card for the hole-in-the-wall but didn't know how to use it. He asked his fellow front rowers, they explained and off he went into Leeds on a night out and had to use the card for the first time. He placed his card in the slot, typed in his PIN and on the screen came, 'Account in order, please state the amount required'. Our prop looked up and down the street, bent forward and said into the screen, 'Twenty-five pounds, please'.

'BRIAN THE CONE'

The Aussies are great ones for nicknames and invariably they identify the person named absolutely spot on. The one and only all time great, Wally Lewis was 'Gator' after the TV cartoon character 'Wallygator'. Wally Fullerton-Smith, who played at Headingley for me and was an international forward, was 'Gator Two'. The fabulous Eric Grothe was 'The Guru' and his Parramatta partner who came with him, Neil Hunt, was 'Guilty' because he had a permanent look of doing something he shouldn't have. Tony Currie the Aussie international who also coached at London Broncos was simply TC and the late super player, Peter Jackson, was

'Action'. Canterbury Bankstown and Hunslet international forward was 'Cement' and when my loose forward at Leeds, Dave Heron, heard about this he demanded to be called 'Fibreglass'!

Coaches too earn nicknames but the one that stands out to me was an English coach who went on to great things as a first team coach and later as an assistant coach at various clubs. It was at one of his first jobs in charge and considering this man was of noted intelligence it rather surprised me. The club was a lowly one but the players were sharp as tacks when, on setting up a series of skills grids in which to work, our coach, who we will call 'Brian', found out that he was one cone short to set up his final grid, so he stood in for the cone for the duration of the one and a half hour session. For ever he is and will be 'Brian the Cone'!

But better to be known as 'Brian the Cone' than not to be known at all as was the case when, as the Great Britain coach I was asked to make some end of season presentations to that superb producer of junior players, Crigglestone ARLFC.

The other Guest of Honour that night was that wonderful sports writer and top journalist, Frank Taylor, who was one of the survivors of the terrible Manchester United air disaster in Munich. Now as the national team coach I had to be in reasonable nick, fitness wise, and on this night had scrubbed up with a new suit, thick dark hair slicked back and, at 5'11" and around 14 stone, at least I looked the part.

Dear Frank was considerably older than me, was about 5'6" tall and weighed in at a rotund 16 stone, was balding and, bless him, because of his dreadful injuries at Munich, walked with a pronounced limp. As we were stood talking about sport in general, I noticed out of the corner of my eye, two of the Under-14s stealthily approaching us carrying autograph books. They stopped about a yard away, nervously building up their courage to ask us to sign their books and unfortunately I heard their conversation. 'That's Maurice Bamford the Great Britain coach' said one of the kids, 'Oh.'

said the other, 'Which one is he?'

Talk about knocking your ego, what!

ANONYMOUS

A well known Lancashire county hooker, who played in Super League up to year four, passed his driving test and bought himself a nice, clean used car. He knew nothing at all about the workings of the engine, its upkeep or the legalities of the tyre treads, absolutely nothing. He phoned a team mate, who was clued up on motors, to come around to his house to give the gleaming vehicle the once-over.

The hooker asked several questions about oil, petrol and general maintenance and then said, 'I know I have to look at my tyres now and again'. His mate nodded and said, 'Yes, around 32 pounds each one'. The hooker looked shocked, 'What' he exploded. 'If I had known they were as expensive as that I wouldn't have bought the bloody thing!'

Hello, anyone at home?

COLD HANDS, WARM HEART

Christmas 1984 saw me coaching at Leeds and I called in to the supporters club at the back of the South Stand for a pint after training. There on the club notice board were the results of the Featherstone Rovers Grand Christmas Draw, as several books of tickets had been sold at Headingley at a recent match. I thought 'there will be some good prizes here, a colour TV or maybe even a week in the Bahamas'. But on note pad paper and written in pencil it said, *Fev Rovers Xmas Draw. 1st Prize: Fish and Chip supper for two at Joe's Fish Shop, Fev, no. 2571. 2nd Prize: Fish and Chips for one, same shop, no. 1335. 3rd Prize: A pair of motor cycle gauntlets no. 784.*

I thought, pity the poor bloke riding through Featherstone on a snowy winters night with cold hands!

Happy days at Fev.

10

SECOND ROWERS

FRANK BIRKIN

Every position on the field in a rugby league team tends to produce characters, that's the nature of the grand old game and it seems to me that the players who are involved more in the game – forwards and half-backs – produce the most of them. Big, rough, tough forwards are remembered with a smile, cheeky little half-backs bring a warm feeling and possibly the Dougie Greenall's, Alan Davis's, Lewis Jones's, Eric Ashton's and Gary Schofield's are thought of as being worth ten bob to watch, so too the Brian Bevan's, Mick Sullivan's and Billy Boston's. But it is the big men that are usually remembered best, particularly from when the game was played in winter.

My earliest of memories watching the game as a small boy was of clouds of steam rising above twelve enormous men, wrestling and striving for possession of the ball from a scrum. Muddy players, unrecognisable yet magnificent, scruffy and untidy yet majestic, and to stand, as a kid, in the darkening winter evenings outside the dressing room door and feel the heat from the deep, hot bath and hear the humour and laughter and be almost able to join in the warmth of the camaraderie, if in spirit only, that one felt even outside in the cold.

These were the warriors, who in my youth were the men who had battled through five years of all out war, and had returned to do battle again on the field of play. The magnificently built, Sammy Newbound of Hunslet, the awesome Dai Prosser of Leeds and there was Frank McManus of Castleford, a huge prop who a friend of mine swore to his dying day he once saw jump off a moving tram in City Square, Leeds, put out his arm to stop himself, and took 50 yards of iron railings with him. These were men of myth and legend, men of deeds spoken of in awe by lesser mortals, such as myself and all my school mates.

Such a God-like man was the fearsome Frank Birkin, 6'6" tall and 17 stone. A man, it was said, who would rather have a fight than his dinner! Big Frank was a landlord at a pub in Bradford and, rumour has it, he was awakened one night and on going downstairs caught a burglar red-handed behind his bar. Frank gave the villain a good hiding and threw him out, then thought to himself, hey, who is going to pay for the window he smashed to get in, so he went outside, pulled the burglar again, cracked him and took £5 from him to pay for the damages.

The burglar served a summons on Frank for theft and the big man was found guilty!

Now Frank was renowned for having a very short fuse and the old adage of 'No sooner a word than a blow' could have been written for him. Frank died years later and was buried in Bradford, where a mate of mine, taking a short cut through a cemetery in the City, found Frank's grave. He told me that he knew it was Frank's resting place because on the head stone it only had one sentence, which read 'Who the bloody hell are you looking at?'

A tremendously hard and courageous forward, Frank had spells at Halifax, Castleford, Salford and Bramley. But it was with the Castleford club that Frank, whilst playing against the Australian tourists, took on, and beat, the fearsome Roy Bull, the tough Aussie prop.

They do say that 'time and distance lends enchantment' and friends of mine who saw that game recon the fight lasted all of twenty minutes! Nevertheless Frank Birkin was some man!

ANONYMOUS

I had a player who as a tough back rower was second to none. Every game he brought his partner, who was called, Beverley, to the match and everyone thought Beverley was his wife. At the end of season presentations, everyone got a shock when the forward turned up with a totally different young lady who, it was found out, was his wife. Beverley, nowhere to be seen, was his 'bit-on-the-side'. So with all the players walking on eggshells around the couple, two of our players who had been out for a few pints arrived late and seeing our forward sat at a table, went over to have a word.

'Hiya' said one of the lads, half looking at the unknown guest of our forward, and mainly through habit of seeing Beverley, said, 'Where's Beverley?'

Now our very streetwise forward never batted an eyelid, he just reached over for his pint and said, 'Near Hull!' and the subject was never broached again that night! Straight John Bull true, and the lad is sadly no longer with us as he died at a very early age, and I am certain, knowing the son of a gun, that he would smile if I said he would have gone much sooner if their lass had ever found out about Beverley!

MARTIN HODGSON

I had the pleasure and privilege to meet this wonderful forward when he was an elderly gentleman at a game at the old Station Road ground at Swinton when looking at a couple of players for the Great Britain Under-21s side. Although an elder statesman of the game the mighty Cumbrian was still a big man and for all his years in Lancashire still maintained that lovely soft Cumbrian accent as he related several stories of that tough, rugged game of rugby league as it was played in those far off days.

A mark of his greatness is that Martin made two tours of Australia, under the captaincy of the wonderful Jim Sullivan in 1932, then again in 1936 with fellow Cumbrian, Jim Brough, as skipper. Signed as a teenager from Cumbrian Rugby Union by Swinton, Martin was an immediate success and indeed was selected for his native county in the inter-county championship not long after signing for the Lions.

He told me of the tradition of big, tough, strong Cumbrian forwards and how, on being selected for the county as a youngster, standing 6'3" and weighing around sixteen and a half stone, he was given the nickname of 'Tiny'. I asked if the name was given to him because he was the youngest in the team and he replied, sincerely, 'No Maurice, it was because I was the smallest in the pack'.

Martin was a world famous goal-kicker too and with his powerful build and the old 'toe end' style could propel the ball a prodigious length. He is still credited with the longest goal in the games history, when he booted that old, heavy, leather ball over the crossbar at the old Recreation Ground, Rochdale to register a penalty goal. An official measurement was taken immediately after the match and the phenomenal distance of 75 yards 3 inches was recorded.

The next time you are stood on a rugby field, stand around 20 metres from a try line and turn around. The crossbar at the far end is what Martin Hodgson kicked that ball over. Unbelievable but very, very true. I spoke to Martin about his world record kick and with total modesty he explained, 'It wasn't as difficult as people make out because I had a breeze behind me and that helped'. His final words to me, on the last time I saw him were, 'I was 17 years old when I came to Swinton from home and I've enjoyed every single moment'.

The late and very great Martin Hodgson.

JACK ARKWRIGHT

When he was playing for Warrington no one could say 'Arkwright' without following it immediately with 'Miller'. Arkwright and Miller, it rolled off the tongue like 'Champagne and Caviar' or 'New Cake and Best Butter'.

Johnny Miller was a hard, tough prop who caused such a stir with his uncompromising play amongst the Aussie supporters on the old, famous hill on the Sydney Cricket Ground, that during a Test Match they dug a 'grave' for him on the Hill.

Jack Arkwright was Johnny Miller's mate, and when necessary they looked after each other. They were Test Match pals, both at the time played at Wilderspool in the Primrose and Blue of the famous Warrington club. Now on the 1936 tour of Australia and New Zealand, the Aussies took the First Test by 24 points to 8 in Sydney before a 64,000 crowd, and the ex-boxer and real tough prop Ray Stehr imposed himself on the British team with a hard display that caught the tourists cold. After doing a real demolition job on the British pack, Stehr was sent off along with Nat Silcock of Widnes but the damage had been done by that time.

Before the Second Test at Brisbane, the tour manager, Mr W Popplewell of Bramley, asked for a volunteer to see to Mr Stehr, 'as early as possible'. Jack Arkwright held up his hand and introduced himself to Ray Stehr at the second scrum. Goodbye Mr Stehr! And the Brits won 12 points to 7.

The Third and deciding Test was played again in Sydney, and a crowd of 54,000 saw a running battle between the two hard men, Arkwright and Stehr, culminating in the pair being sent off after an all-out humdinger of a scrap. Jack Arkwright had done the job again, getting rid of the dangerous prop and Britain went on to win the game, again

12 points to 7 and with it the Ashes, by two Tests to one.

Jack Arkwright was a very big and powerful man and he maintained his size and upright smartness throughout his life. His son, young Jack, was a hard forward himself and grandson Chris was an international in his own right.

Like most of the tough men of his era, Jack Arkwright was superb company and I had the pleasure of sitting at the table with him and the former great St Helens wingman, Alf Ellaby at a dinner in Lancashire. The conversation, obviously, centred on the game and Alf, reminiscing with Jack, asked the big man, 'What was the team we played in London at the White City Stadium Jack?'

Jack smiled and said 'Streatham and Mitcham'.

Alf looked in amazement, 'What a good memory you have' he said to Jack.

'Aye and I remember their loose forward's name as well, it was Felton,' replied the big ex forward, 'and the reason I remember him is that we played them twice that season and I had to chastise him twice!'

Jack was a landlord for many years and no one created any trouble in big Jack's pub.

The superb, late Jack Arkwright.

SONNY WHAKARAU

This excellent second rower was a native Kiwi, a Maori warrior in every sense. An absolute dream to handle Sonny gave 100% where ever he played or who ever he played for.

I first saw Sonny when he had just arrived here in the UK from Wellington, New Zealand. He had paid his own way over and had landed at the Batley club and was showing what he could do in an A team game at the old Crown Flatts ground against Dewsbury A.

He was outstanding in the game and afterwards I checked

to see if he had signed on at Mount Pleasant. He said that he had given his word to play in this game and to wait until the board had chance to discuss him on the Tuesday evening meeting. He phoned me on Wednesday to say that Batley had offered him fair terms and he was going to keep his word and play the season out with them. Fair enough. The lad had been straight with both me and Batley.

Sonny went home in the close season and I left Dewsbury and went to Bramley. One day I received a phone call from New Zealand and it was Sonny, asking if I could find an opening at Bramley for him, I said yes and Sonny came over. He had recently married in Wellington and the problem of accommodation arose. We, like most second division clubs, did not have a lot of money so we had to scout around to find the best we could afford. A little terraced house in the Meanwood area of Leeds popped up from nowhere and although it was not the most chic of houses, it was clean, tidy and warm.

Sonny worked with me on the ground staff at Mclaren Field and made an immediate impact on the side with his hard running and tough tackling. The team did well in Sonny's first season and we gained promotion into what was called the 'Hetherington Plan', a middle league idea from the then Sheffield Eagles boss, Gary Hetherington, that was aimed to help the 'yo-yo' clubs – the ones not quite good enough for the first division but too good for the second – and the two clubs that went up were Huddersfield and Bramley.

Sonny came back for another season and his contract this time included better accommodation and a car! The house this time was in Bramley but the sponsorship for a car fell through. After about a month, Sonny was getting desperate and I had a word with Jeff Wine, our chairman, and he agreed that Sonny could buy a car and we would pay for it on the 'tick'.

To be fair to Sonny, the car he chose was a banger in every sense of the word, in fact calling it a banger was overestimating it, it really was a pile of junk. To give an idea how bad it was, an absolute essential was to carry two bricks in the boot. These were inserted behind, or in front of the tyres depending which way the vehicle was facing on a hill and a hammer was often needed to tap the carburettor to clear the dirt out of it before the beast would start!

Sonny came late at one home game and in his rush to the dressing rooms, forgot the bricks when he parked in the club car park. On his return the car was gone but about 20 yards across the car park was a jagged hole in the fence behind which was a six foot drop into spare land and that was the final resting place, bricks and all, of the Whakarau limousine. I can't imagine any Super League star driving around in that embarrassment for a vehicle but the Maori warrior did, and enjoyed it.

Sonny went onto bigger things at Doncaster, Keighley and Wakefield before returning to the island of the long white cloud, New Zealand.

ARTHUR CLUES

I suppose as kids we all have heroes. I know that all the heroes that figured in my youth were rugby league players and the biggest all-time hero of mine was an Australian ex-policeman from Sydney who just happened to be, in my opinion, the finest second row forward ever, Arthur Clues.

Big Arthur – to all who saw this 21-year-old stride onto the Headingley pitch that winter Saturday afternoon in 1946 – well over 6 feet and weighing around 15 stone, had played in all three Tests for Australia against the 1946 tourists, along with the wonderful duo of Pat Devery and Lionel Cooper who graced the famous Claret and Gold jerseys of the Huddersfield club.

In those three Test Matches, Arthur had several fights with Doug Phillips, the Oldham and later Belle Vue Rangers second rower, and the big centre from Bradford Northern, Jack Kitchen. Arthur was sent off in one Test after an altercation with big Doug and received a suspension despite claiming that he was sent off for nothing. To which the Aussie committee said: 'We know; we are giving you three matches for missing the pommy bastard!'

Anyone who saw the big Aussie, either as a young player at Leeds or when he moved to Hunslet in his later years was very lucky indeed. He was poetry in motion. Quick for a big man, he could side step, swerve and had a hand-off like the kick of a mule. He had the sweetest left-footed kick one could wish to see, either long raking touch finders or the deftest of little chips over an advancing defence and regather on the run. His tackling was a devastating, bone shaking experience and he was tough, very tough.

As a kid I used to go to sleep wishing to wake up as Arthur Clues. I graduated into a second rower because of him; I copied everything he did on the field. He was and still is my hero.

Now a sure way of estimating a players standing in the game is to listen to the opposition supporters cat-calling a player, almost hating him, then should that player move to their club, he is an immediate hero to them. That was big Arthur, hated by opposing fans, yet admired by them all. He was resident in Leeds from his arrival in 1946 to the time of his death only a few short years ago and never lost the Aussie twang in his accent. In much later years Arthur used to pop in to see me when I was employed as the Leeds commercial manager and I used to ask him if he practised his accent!

There are hundreds of super tales about the man who was a legend in the City of Leeds and one that tells just how much he was respected and feared is told by a former Halifax player when Arthur was at the back end of his career at

Hunslet.

Halifax had a big, hard pack whose battles with the similar six from the Boulevard, Hull, are recorded in the games folklore. Each member of the Thrum Hall pack could have been the heavyweight champion of the world if they hadn't played our game, they were awesome.

So the scene was set, Halifax v Hunslet at Thrum Hall and the *Halifax Courier* carried headlines 2 inches high, 'Clues calls it a day after Saturday's clash at Thrum Hall'. This was going to be the ogres last match; the man who had terrorised all teams for years was calling it a day. Retribution time was here, and so it was. Arthur gave back as much as he received but the odds were overwhelming and he took the mother and father of good hidings. Not that he whinged about it for he had handed it out over the years and he could take it too.

When the whistle went to end the game, in true rugby league tradition all the Halifax team shook his hand and wished him well in his retirement. So his fabulous career had ended, but had it? Halifax had to go to Parkside to play Hunslet in the league and it was the last match of the season. The Thrum Hall dressing room was full of copies of the latest *Halifax Courier* as the players read, 'Clues returns for Halifax clash!' The players were deathly silent, they could not believe their eyes. Then, one by one they commented, 'Well he must know that I did not lay a finger on him' and 'I never touched him, he's always been my mate' and so on.

The day came and Big Arthur went through them like the proverbial dose of salts. There were black eyes and burst noses everywhere and when the final whistle sounded it was Arthur who went around to all the Halifax bloodied players and said, 'Well played boys, now you can enjoy my retirement' and he went from the game for ever but who can forget the smiling larger than life Aussie who was a credit to our game and made Leeds his home.

11

LOOSE FORWARDS

FROM BILLY JUKES TO ANDY FARRELL

The men who wore the number 13 jersey were always classed as the link between forwards and backs. Usually the loose forward was a good footballer, but on occasions a player operated there because of his defensive prowess, but overall the last man down had pace and was a good leader.

On the first ever tour in 1910 three tests were played, two against Australia, both in Sydney, and one in Auckland against the Kiwis and three different loose forwards were used, A Avery (Oldham), W Winstanley (Leigh) and Billy Jukes (Hunslet).

Jukes scored the first hat trick of tries by a forward in an Anglo-Australian Test Match in the First Test and he played at blind side prop in that game, a feat so far still a record. The Great Britain side of that era played in jerseys of red and white hoops and as the first two Tests were won by the tourists, the Third Test was replaced by a combined Australia/New Zealand v Great Britain match, in Sydney, which ended in a 13–all draw, played in front of a 50,000 crowd.

On the 1914 tour, the redoubtable Cumbrian style wrestling champion, Douglas Clark of Huddersfield was the last man down in all three Tests against the Aussies and was a hero amongst heroes in the famous final Test in Sydney in which the tourists were reduced to 10 men throughout all the second half and for a spell, down to nine men as injury upon injury took its toll, but emerged as history making champions with a 14 points to 6 victory against all the odds. This Test match went down in folklore as 'The Rorke's Drift Test', named after the valiant defence of a hospital station by a handful of British soldiers against thousands of Zulu warriors.

In the one Test in New Zealand our number 13 was L Clampitt (Broughton Rangers). The First World War disrupted the scheduled 1918 tour but international tours resumed in 1920, with the tourists in an all white strip and the 'pocket battleship', Frank Gallagher, then of Dewsbury, was loose man in all three Aussie Tests and H Hilton (Oldham) in all three Tests in New Zealand.

In 1924, Gallagher, now a Batley player, was again at loose forward in four of the six Tests against the Aussies and the Kiwis, and stand-off in the other two. Joe Thompson (Leeds) and J Price (Wigan) played in the two games that Gallagher was at number six. In the Third Test in Brisbane, Gallagher became the first tourist ever to be sent off in the 21 points to 11 defeat, but the Ashes were won in a two Tests to one series, and this tour saw the Great Britain side in the now customary white jersey with the Red and Blue 'V' for the first time.

Frank Gallagher, now at Leeds, was selected for a record-breaking third tour but had to withdraw and the great Bill Horton (Wakefield Trinity) played in all six Tests at loose man. This was the series that saw the Aussies wear the famous Green and Gold for the first time, before that playing in the Maroon and Blue of the two league playing states of Queensland and New South Wales.

1932 saw Joe Thompson (Leeds) make his third consecutive tour – the only forward to play in three Ashes winning sides on tour – with the number 13 jersey shared between, Jack Feetham (Salford) four times, Martin Hodgson (Swinton) once and A Fildes (St Helens) once.

Harry Beverley (Hunslet) had the 13 shirt in the three Tests against the Aussies in 1936 and L Troup (Barrow) wore it in the two Tests against the Kiwis.

The tourists sailed on the aircraft carrier, *HMS Indomitable*, in 1946 and the exciting runner Ike Owens (Leeds) was the loose man in all three against Australia and the one in Auckland.

As we now come into the 1950s we are approaching the era of superb footballers who donned the 13 shirt – although some clubs would not wear the number 13, instead their loose forwards would carry 14, fearing bad luck!

Almost every club had a cracking loose man. Wigan, a priceless side in this period, signed Bill Hudson from Batley and Les White from York. White, better known as a second rower, could fit easily into the 13 spot with his skilful play and while Hudson's strong suit was his bone-buckling defence, he knew his way around the field all right. But for me it was Billy Blan who was the top footballer at Central Park. Brother Albert was a good player too, but Billy was the master tactician and technician and was superbly built for the job.

From the late 1940s through into the '50s Hunslet produced two class loose forwards in Des Clarkson and Ken Traill. Clarkson, a Castleford lad, was a smart ball player, with a good kicking game and was one of the most superbly turned out players one could wish to see. Wonderfully built, with immaculate blond hair, and always with spotless white ankle bandages perfectly turned over about 2 inches above his highly polished football boots. And his game was just that, polished! A great icon for a youngster to copy, this lad from a mining background in Airedale, also had spells besides

Hunslet, at Leeds, Halifax, Leigh and Keighley. A formidable opponent but I found him a nice man with a vast amount of football knowledge and his passing a few years ago left the game poorer for it.

So too Ken Traill, a Northumberland born lad who learned his rugby league in the Hunslet schools, again sadly recently deceased. Ken was another classical handling loose forward who was given his first chance at the home of so many good players, Parkside, Hunslet. Indeed his father was a well known local forward and his brother, Andy, played for years at Keighley. Ken Traill, the peerless passer of the ball made both the 1950 and the 1954 tours as a Bradford Northern player and later took the well trod path to Thrum Hall, Halifax and finally to Wakefield Trinity and further fame as a very successful coach of the Trinity club.

Ken also played a part in the cult film, *This Sporting Life*, written by David Storey and staring Richard Harris. The film was shot at Wakefield's Belle Vue ground when Ken was coaching there and the director must have spotted Ken's obvious talents and gave him a part. Ken was just that, talented. A natural footballer who knew the game inside out.

Whilst speaking of Wakefield Trinity and Ken Traill, I must give a mention to a loose man that was as respected as any in the game at that period, Trinity's Len Bratley. A tough, old-fashioned, hard-playing forward with a fearless attitude to the game. Len's best years must have been swallowed up in the Second World War but he operated just before the outbreak and was firing on all cylinders after peace was declared. A grand player and one you would want on your side.

Ken Traill's tandem partner on the 1950 tour at loose forward was another superb footballer and a gentleman to boot, Harry Street. A Lancashire lad, Harry's silky skills at number 13, backed up by brother Arthur's no nonsense defence and hard attitude in the second row, was a major factor in Dewsbury's climb to prominence in the late 1940s and his subsequent move to Wigan in the early 1950s brought this excellent player into a well deserved limelight. A move back into Yorkshire, to Leeds, saw Harry Street earn a Wembley winners medal in 1957 when he locked the scrum for the Headingley club in the victory over Barrow.

About this time a young back rower from the Borders of Scotland took the professional ticket and without any fuss came down to Huddersfield to become a legend in the game. He went with Ken Traill, as the other number 13, on the 1954 tour and played in four of the six Tests with Ken playing in the other two. He was, of course, Dave Valentine. Huddersfield was to be Dave's only club and in his day, with being a Scot, he was qualified to play for the Other Nationalities in the European representative games against England, France and Wales. The back three partnership for the 'Exiles' was a coach's dream, Clues (Leeds), Bath (Warrington) and Valentine (Huddersfield), a world class back row.

From the late 1950s, things were stirring around the league in the loose forward department as good players moved from the slightly lesser clubs to the big guns. Derek Turner left Hull Kingston Rovers for Oldham, the evergreen 'Gentleman' John Whiteley was developing quickly behind an awesome Hull pack and the ultra tough Vince Karalius was knocking on the door at Saints. Wigan too had uncovered a belting number 13 in Roy Evans who would take the game by storm in a couple of seasons. Brian Shaw, the Hunslet prop or back rower moved across the City of Leeds and up the hill to Headingley and around the corner was the cool Hunslet, Hull Kingston Rovers and Leeds player, Harry Poole. So things looked good in the loose forward sector, especially as the game approached the most successful tour for many, many years in 1970, but before that there was the tour of 1958 which was captained by Alan Prescott of Saints, a man who would enter the Lions *Hall of Fame* for his heroic deeds.

The 1958 tour saw two of the finest loose forwards ever to grace the game make the trip, John Whiteley and Vince (Vinty) Karalius. So good were the pair that a place had to be found for them both. Whiteley played at loose man in the First Test, when Great Britain were beaten by 25 points to 8. Then in the second and third Aussie Tests Karalius was at 13, gaining much notoriety and the nickname the Aussies gave him that stuck forever, 'the Wild Bull of the Pampas', with Whiteley operating in the second row. It was in the Second Test in Brisbane that captain and prop forward, Alan Prescott, cemented a place for himself in the folklore history of the game when, despite suffering a severe broken arm in the fourth minute of the game, he played on for the full 80 minutes and bravely led his side to a famous 25 to 18 victory. What made the win so historic was that in the 15th minute, star stand-off, Dave Bolton (Wigan) was taken off with a broken collar bone. Neither Prescott or Bolton played again on tour but the Ashes were taken by the Lions with a superb 40 points to 17 win in the final Test in Sydney. This tour was another first in British/Australasian Tests when Hull's Welsh hooker Tommy Harris missed the First Test against the Kiwis in Auckland it was the first time that a touring side had played a Test without a Welshman in the side.

The 1962 touring side took the all round skills of the young Wigan sensation, Roy Evans, and the tough, wonderful leader, Derek 'Rocky' Turner who by now had left Oldham to become a cornerstone of the fabulous Wakefield Trinity side. A good mate of mine, Billy Slater, who was a half-back for Hunslet and Doncaster, tells of playing at the old Tattersfield ground against Trinity and being told by his coach that Derek had a weakness in that he was slow breaking out of the scrum near the touchline, therefore a blind side break was on if a nippy half-back got a good, quick heel from a set scrum. Billy was quick and his luck was in as away he shot from the scrum base and the blind side was wide open. A run of 40 yards was halted by the Trinity full back and Billy had to wait until just before half-time for another chance to attack the blind side, but run it he did and as he sailed away, again with no Derek Turner in sight, the lights suddenly went out as he was knocked senseless by a sledge hammer tackle from the loose forward. As Billy was coming back into the land of the living, he heard Derek Turner say, 'I don't fall for the same trick twice', and Billy never went blind side against Mr Turner again!

The late, great Roy Evans retired early, and took a place on the board of directors with a Lancashire team. As a board member, he attended a coaching course as a pupil, at the Crystal Palace Sports Centre at which I was on staff. On the course was our old mate, Terry Dewhirst. Terry was paired up with Roy, who must have been three stones out of playing condition, in a tackling exercise. Terry wasn't in bad nick but the ex-international and top loose forward still had a bit left and rounded Terry twice, firstly with a swerve and then with a heavy hand off. When it came to Roy's turn to tackle, he felled Terry, like a giant Redwood, twice, with copybook ankle tackles that turned the clock back and big Terry had to take seconds from the sadly missed gentleman, Roy Evans.

On the 1962 tour, of the five Tests played, Derek Turner played in four at 13 and Warrington's Laurie Gilfedder in one. The tour of 1966 was captained by a loose forward, that grand leader Harry Poole, playing for Leeds at the time. But Harry was injured early in the tour and did not play in a Test in Australia, leading into the old chestnut, 'Which captain went to Australia and never played in a Test? Why, Captain

Cook of course.' The man who played 13 in all the five Tests was Swinton's Dave Robinson.

In 1970, arguably the best ever touring team left these shores. The success of this excellent side caused a rethink in the way the game was played and coached Down Under and money was poured into the Aussie game through the Rothman's Sports Grants. But the biggest change was in the ideas that the guru of Aussie coaching, Jack Gibson, brought over from American grid-iron football. Jack's initiative revolutionised the whole concept of training and coaching techniques in Australia and the newly constructed Australian Coaching Scheme accepted his suggestions and moved the game forward at an incredible speed. This was because after their success in the 1966 tour, the Aussies expected to wipe the floor with our 1970 boys and it didn't go to plan. Hence the complete blueprint was changed, good young players were plucked from clubs and given advanced fitness and skills training in preparation for international selection and needless to say, the Aussies have gone on from there.

The two excellent loose forwards on the 1970 tour were Doug Laughton, the Wigan lock and the outstanding back rower of his era, Castleford's Malcolm Reilly, who played at 13 in all six Tests. Under the old competitive scrimmaging rules and the five yards on-side rule at the play the ball which allowed far more tactical play and close support work, the tourists' pack was indeed awesome. The front row in the majority of the Tests was Dennis Hartley (Castleford), Tony Fisher (Bradford Northern) and Cliff Watson (Saints). Old timers will no doubt rub their hands and smile softly at the thought of these giants of their day. Further smiles, I'm sure, when we look at the back three, Doug Laughton (Wigan), Jimmy Thompson (Featherstone Rovers) and Mal Reilly, what a pack!

Of the six Tests, three in Australia and three in New

Zealand, Great Britain lost only one, the First Test in Brisbane. But the successes of the 1970 squad had severe repercussions as to our standing in rugby league world rankings, as the Aussies new coaching and development plan kicked in and, frankly, they've been ahead of us ever since! This was evident on the 1974 tour when Great Britain lost the Ashes, albeit very closely, by two Tests to one. The two 13s on that tour were the superb, skilful and tough, George Nicholls of Saints and the man said by many to be the second Malcolm Reilly, Castlford's Steve 'Knocker' Norton. George Nicholls was at loose forward in all six Tests.

The 1979 tour included an unprecedented 33 players in the squad, including three hookers with the two 13s of Norton, then at Hull and the grand footballer, Mick Adams of Widnes. Adams had four Tests in the 13 shirt and Norton, two but the Tourists were thrashed three to nil on the Aussie leg and lost one of the three in New Zealand.

Seven Tests were played on the trip of 1984, the normal six in Australia and New Zealand and a first time Test at Mount Hagen in Papua New Guinea. Great Britain were whitewashed in both major Test series, six to nil but won in Mount Hagen by 38 points to 20. Three men wore the 13 shirt, Mick Adams (Widnes), Mick Worrall (Oldham) and Terry Flanagan (Oldham).

In the period since 1984 the loose forward position has been dominated by only four players: Ellery Hanley (Wigan and Leeds), Phil Clarke (Wigan), Mike Gregory (Warrington) and Andy Farrell (Wigan) and a few other players who, it seems, could not quite provide that indescribable spark as did, particularly, Hanley and Clarke.

Having browsed through the touring sides viewing the best loose forwards, as one would consider a player being selected to tour as the best around at the time. And needless to say, from Avery and Jukes in 1910 through to Clarke and Farrell in 2004, what a great selection of super players, each one brilliant in some way, many household names in their day, each one crowd pleasers. But it would be remiss of me not to mention most of the players who wore the 'Glamour' jersey of number 13 since the 1980s. Andy Goodway of Wigan played in quite a few Tests at loose forward and to a lesser degree, Gary Divorty (Hull) and Ian Potter (Wigan), whilst Harry Pinner of Saints, did a wonderful job for me at both loose forward and captain in the 1985 series against the Kiwis and France. Andy Platt (Saints), Paul Dixon (Leeds), Michael Jackson (Wakefield Trinity), Les Holliday (Widnes), Chris Joynt (Saints), Dave Heron (Leeds), Mick Crane (Hull), Len Casey (Hull KR) and Dave Hall (Hull KR) have all served their country with distinction in the crucial position of 'last man down', but since his debut in 1993 against the Kiwis, the man in possession of that cherished number 13 has been, mostly, Andy Farrell (Wigan).

I have been fortunate to come across many of the players mentioned here in my years of involvement in the game and the common denominator is that these men, full of character and bravery, were in the most part, part-time players. Lads who held down full-time jobs and played the game in their spare hours. This point is one that must be remembered in tandem with the stories of heroism and humour of the days when only the odd game each season was shown on TV and our beloved game was played, very strictly, in the 'M62 corridor'. Sky TV and Super League have brought our game forward tremendously and full-time employment in the game, unheard of and unthought of for so many years, has been a revelation, but at what cost? So much change, so quickly, must have a long lasting effect on the principles and traditions that we, of my era, were taught. Could it kill the characters that this wonderful game once produced in abundance?

12

THE DIRECTORS

HARRY JEPSON

The governing body of the game was the Rugby League Council. This Council was made up by a representative of each club, usually the club chairman and from this various sub-committees were selected. The Management Committee was most powerful, dealing with almost every thing from international match decisions to domestic football rulings, then the County Committees, representing the three Counties on the administration of the old Yorkshire and Lancashire County Cups, the selection of the teams for the Inter-County Championship and all the intricate and political negotiations needed to satisfy the requirements of thirty odd clubs, three Counties and the thirty-odd individuals in the shape of the club chairmen, each and all wanting what they considered the best for their club (and not necessarily for the good of the game).

Then there was the Disciplinary Committee who decided on the validity of the sending off of players that occurred from time to time, and handed out the suspensions that each case merited. This membership of the inner sanctum of the game was a staunchly guarded, all male stronghold as hardly any females were allowed on boards of directors, and, certainly only a very few boardrooms allowed ladies admittance after matches when the male directors met to discuss that day's game and carry out that essential function, lobbying, before the next Council meeting.

My earliest recollection of a lady being allowed into the inner sanctum of the Council Chamber at the Rugby League Headquarters was when Mrs Kathy Hetherington, as chairperson of the Sheffield Eagles club, challenged the objections by the Council at that time, and won the right to represent her club at the meetings, and good for her!

One must look too at the various men who formed the Council. Some were very wealthy businessmen and involved in high finance, some were in business but not as high profile as some of the others. Then there were headmasters and school teachers, plumbers and joiners, retired local council officers, there were bakers and Royal Mail workers, in fact every cross section of life that there could be. The reason for such a mixed box of tricks was that, not too long ago, a lot of the clubs in the Rugby Football League were in fact members clubs. That is, very much like the Working Men's Clubs of today, where they became a paid-up member at their rugby league club and stood for election at the annual club meeting. If elected they would be asked to put up a bond of anything from £500 to as low as £100. Of course this was a substantial sum in those days but no money was actually stumped up as it was a signed promise to pay up that amount should the club require it.

A club that was a limited company would need more than that though and at this sort of club a board member may have been asked to 'chip in' for the transfer of a player to the club, but as a company, any input of money would be returned at the financial year-end, just as in any business.

Any club hoping for admission into the league today has to produce a business plan, indicating capital resources, supporter base details, plus have a ground and facilities to a high standard, as described in the League's publication *Framing the Future*, and at least a ten-year outlook showing capital growth.

There are a few places on certain clubs' boards that are filled by men who offer technical skills or experience other than any financial input, but today these places are few and far between. I personally worked with quite a few chairmen and boards of directors who were, taking everything into consideration, mostly decent blokes. Some were not though and at one of my earlier clubs I was approached by the vice-chairman who asked why I was considering bringing a player from another club to join us. 'Do you rate him?' he asked. I told him that I did and he replied 'Oh, I don't rate him; all he can do is score tries and kick goals'.

Not all directors were like him, thank goodness! One of my better, much better, chairmen was Harry Jepson who had seen just about everything in rugby league and was generally accepted as the most knowledgeable man in the game. Harry was the perfect chairman with whom to work as he supported the coach in every aspect and his experience was priceless. A retired headmaster, Harry was another from the game's heartland, Hunslet, having been born and bred in that area of heavy industry, south of the River Aire, in Leeds.

Harry was first and foremost a rugby league man. A student of the game, Harry tells of how he remembers as a small child being taken to the end of their street by his Grandma, to watch the Hunslet team return from winning the old Yorkshire Cup, in the pouring rain, with the team in a horse-drawn wagon and the driver wearing a hessian sack around his shoulders to protect him from the weather.

Harry joined the Hunslet committee on being demobilised from the Army in 1946 where his old friend and headmaster of the ultra-renowned schools' rugby league team in the area, Hunslet Carr, Mr Edgar Meeks, was at the time the chairman of the famous old club.

Harry helped the much respected secretary, Mr Richardson, as his assistant and he has a mountain of classical tales about the ways of the game in those far-off days, such as the time Mr Richardson told Harry that he was going to reduce a certain player's weekly expenses by a halfpenny as the player could alight from the tram-car one stop further away from the ground on his way from work to training and walk that distance. He explained to Harry, 'The player is only seventeen years old and if he plays until he is thirty, imagine all those halfpennies we will save the club!'

Or the time when the groundsman, who maintained both the Parkside rugby pitch and the adjoining cricket field as if it was his own garden, came into the boardroom when Mr Meeks was entertaining the touring French club side at Parkside.

'The Hunslet lasses are fornicating with these "Froggies," Mr Meeks,' he reported.

'It's all right, there's no harm to come from it,' replied the chairman.

'Oh there is Mr Meeks. There's two of them on't wicket,' said the irate groundsman.

Another great tale that Harry picked up as a young man was from a club helper at the turn of the century, in the days of the world-class player Albert Goldthorpe. The club helper was a very religious man who never swore or blasphemed and went to chapel once a day and four times on Sundays. Ward's farm, now an industrial estate, was in those days a series of cornfields just a short walking distance from the Parkside ground. One summers evening the current chairman was in the club office when in burst the religious helper. 'Chairman, I've just seen Albert Goldthorpe in the cornfield on Ward's farm and he's with Amy Jones, alone, the pair of them'.

The chairman said, 'Well Joe, Albert is a single man and both are old enough to behave,' hoping that that would be enough to appease the do-gooder telling tales about the young couple.

'But Albert is supposed to be such a clean living lad' stuttered the helper and the chairman could see that he was on the brink of saying something he would be sorry for later. 'And I knew he was up to something,' he continued, 'because when he saw me he "shate" himself!'

Harry recons that that term must crop up somewhere in the bible.

Harry's vocation as a teacher in the hard environment of the Hunslet schools, amongst children whose parents were not blessed with a lot of money, has left him with some superb tales and one he recalls is of a kid, 'Jimmy,' the kind of kid of whom there is always one in any group, not a bad kid but the kind that strange things happen to!

Now this was just after the 1939–45 war and the school inspectors had not changed from as they had been for many years. One particular inspector, a very sour-faced spinster, who was a stickler for things being correct and would allow zero tolerance, was due at any time. A phone call from one of Harry's school teacher mates told him that she was on her way down to Harry's school and would be there any minute.

Now Jimmy was sat in the front row so that Harry could observe him close by, but Harry didn't want Jimmy sat there when Miss 'Sourpuss' was addressing the class. Jimmy had to be at the rear, unseen. So with everything in place, the inspector rustled into Harry's classroom in the midst of a lesson on Greek mythology, about the defence of a bridge by one lone warrior. The inspector asked the class 'What period of time was the story?'

Only two put their hands up, Jimmy and a little girl, luckily the girl got the nod, 'Greek mythology, miss.' she answered.

'Who was defending the bridge?' was her next poser.

Again Jimmy was ignored and another kid said 'The Greeks, miss.'

Thank goodness thought Harry, then she asked, 'Now children, who was attacking the bridge?' and Jimmy's hand was up in a flash.

Remembering it was 1946 and Jimmy was liable to say anything, Harry cringed, 'Yes, the boy at the back' she said, pointing to Jimmy and with a deep breath Jimmy answered, 'T'Japs, miss'.

Harry's class got by with the skin of their teeth.

Harry spoke fluent French and for years went on international duty as official interpreter to the Great Britain team. When, in my first Test Match as Great Britain coach, we beat the French at Headingley by 50 points to 4, I was naturally delighted and with Harry as the interpreter we attended the after match press meeting. The usual questions were asked, 'How did I feel about the then record score against the French?' and 'What would I do if we lost the return game in Perpignan in three weeks' time?' I was on cloud nine and to the last question I replied, 'If we lose in Perpignan, I will hang myself from the nearest lamp post'. Harry related my sentiments to the French press, verbatim.

We lost in Perpignan! Only just, but we lost. The French demanded a press meeting and as I had gloated a bit at Headingley I had to attend. Yes, there it was waiting for me, just as Harry had explained, a brand new rope tied in a noose and all the French press stood by the window pointing down to the nearest lamp post!

That certainly brought a wry smile to Harry's face!

These days, despite having retired some years ago, Harry is still involved with the game and amongst his many rugby league commitments he is a leading organiser of the annual

Hunslet (Parkside) ex-players' dinners. As an elder statesman of our game he, needless to say, cannot be replaced. A wonderful rugby league ambassador and a superb man, Mr Harry Jepson, OBE.

JEFF WINE

Whilst in my last coaching spell at the grand old Bramley club, my chairman was an absolute gentleman, and along with Harry Jepson, one of the better men I have worked with. Jeff Wine had supported Leeds United for many years but had an affinity with sport in general. His work as a top accountant opened sporting doors all over and this very honest and articulate man had friendships throughout soccer, boxing and rugby.

Jeff and his board of directors at that time were all of the Jewish faith, Ronnie Teeman, Anthony Sugare and Melvin Levi and thereby hangs this next tale.

My assistant coach was a terrific rugby league man, ex Hunslet and Dewsbury scrum half, Ray Abbey. We had a very testing match away to Barrow and Jeff travelled on the bus with the team but Ronnie Teeman and Tony Sugare had to get back to Leeds early so they went up by car. Now one player I feared may do us some damage was the big, strong South Sea Islander, Moses Kolloto, who was in a rich vein of form for the Shipbuilders and was scoring a lot of tries.

We won the game and big Moses Kolloto won Barrow's man of the match award. Ray and I were in the very happy dressing room when Jeff came in to say 'well done' to the lads. He called me over and said, 'How about you and Ray coming for a drink with me in the Barrow boardroom?' We said thanks and went with Jeff to have a natter with the Barrow directors and Jeff felt better not being on his own.

The Barrow chairman looked after us very well and turned to his secretary and said, 'See if you can get our man of the match up into the boardroom to accept his award, please?' Jeff said to me 'Who won their man of the match?' and I answered 'Moses Kolloto'. Jeff thought for a moment and said 'Is he coming up here?' and I said 'Yes, to get his award' and Jeff replied, with a sly smile, 'Teeman and Sugare will be jealous to death. They have gone home, and I am going to meet Moses!'

Jeff was no slouch as a sprinter and I remember one summer evening when our squad at Bramley had trained very hard in pre-season, when for a bit of fun Jeff challenged the whole team to a race over the length of the old McLaren Field ground. He simply took off his coat, rolled up his white shirt sleeves and was ready! All the players were in summer training gear, totally warmed up and I gave them 'Get set, go!'

Now Jeff was in his early forties, hadn't trained for years and was racing that evening against some nippy sprinters who were as fit as they would ever be. He ran an easy third, only behind my two wingmen.

He was full of good ideas for developing team spirit. He would say, 'What do you think of this idea?' and explain his notion. He expected the truth and if the idea was a non-starter, he would want to be told straight, but I honestly had to agree with almost everything he suggested on the team spirit issue. He had a pal who produced discs, the singing, vocal type and he suddenly, without warning, took the whole team to his mate's studio and we recorded the never to be forgotten release, *We Love Rugby League*. It was played twice on Radio Leeds.

Poor record, great guy, Jeff Wine.

BILL HUGHES
Mr Hughes was the chairman at Halifax, when in 1977 he

asked Ronnie Dobson to join the four man board of directors at Thrum Hall. Ronnie had played at Halifax and was then doing well in business, as well as playing amateur rugby league at Dudley Hill, Bradford. Now Halifax at this time had just been beaten at home by the excellent amateur side, Cawood's from Hull, in the John Player Trophy and were entrenched at the bottom of the league with a record of played 22, lost 22. The grand old club were facing extinction, no money, no sponsors, no hope!

Bill Hughes had seen it all at Halifax, as secretary he had been involved in almost every major final with the club, including two visits to Wembley. He had seen the great days and now was staring at the worst. However Mr Hughes should be credited with the greatest honour the Halifax club can give because it was his foresight and good judgement, plus his casting vote to continue as Halifax Rugby League Football Club, when the then New Hunslet wanted to buy out the Halifax club, lock, stock and barrel, and play at Thrum Hall as Hunslet RLFC. Mr Hughes and the board had just engaged me as coach and at that extraordinary board meeting, with the vote locked at two to sell and two to stay, the chairman said, 'I think we are coming to the end of the dark tunnel. I feel we have selected the man, in the new coach, to lead us back into the light and therefore gentlemen I cast my vote to stay!'

It could have so easily gone the other way and the famous old club would have gone for ever. Later, when things were much better and we were at the top of the league and winning games regularly, albeit by drop goals, we, still in division two, beat Wakefield Trinity of the first division, at Thrum Hall in the quarter-final of the Challenge Cup by 7 points to 3.

Johnny Blair dropped four goals for us; Jimmy Birts dropped one and kicked a penalty goal. So from being down and out in two seasons we had turned things around; we had achieved promotion, were Yorkshire Cup finalists and were now in the semi-final of the big one, and all on a shoe-string budget!

Mr Hughes stood on top of the old stone steps leading to the office at Thrum Hall immediately after the Wakefield game and called down to me, 'Would you pop up to see me, Maurice?' and I did, still in my track suit with the mud all over it. He had tears in his eyes as the emotion of the day hit him and he shook my hand gently, 'Maurice, in your short time with us you have done us proud,' then with a smile said, 'but please, Maurice, no more bloody drop goals'.

A gentleman indeed was Mr. Hughes.

RONNIE DOBSON

I met Ronnie when I went to help out at Dudley Hill ARLFC in 1976. Ronnie was a tough prop who had gained professional experience at Hunslet and Halifax and he was in fact the last player to score a try at the old Parkside ground and the comment at that time was 'If Dobby can score a try, then its about time the ground was pulled down!' You've guessed it, Ronnie didn't score many tries.

We were mates from day one, possibly through mutual respect, and when he was approached to join the board at the ailing Halifax RLFC, his first job as football director was to bring me to the club. I went as much as anything for Ronnie but the move worked out well for all concerned.

A huge part of the job at Halifax was to get some spirit back into the old place. Spirit and camaraderie amongst the players was what we were seeking and we hoped that the spirit would flow onto the terraces to create a togetherness not felt at the old ground for a few years. Ronnie, very much the junior board member with the old guard, Bill Boardall, Selwyn Heptinstall and Bill Hughes guiding him through the minefields of football directorship, suggested that the club stand a meal after training for the players and staff. Now it was universally known that there was not much spare cash at the club, so Bill Hughes gave Ronnie explicit instructions 'Not to spend more than £2 per head'. It was virtually impossible to keep to that strict a budget with 17 players and three staff but Ronnie trusted the players to be sensible about their ordering. Lo and behold the total bill came to £245! Ronnie coughed up the money and then phoned Mr Hughes to tell him of the shortfall in the kitty. The chairman had given Ronnie £45 so he had to fork out 200 smackers and Bill Hughes gave him some sound advice on the phone, 'Well Ronnie, you were in charge of the kitty and you overspent. Learn by it, but you will have to stand the shortfall!' So the spirit and camaraderie cost my old mate 200 quid, but he was on the up in those days and took it like a man.

Ronnie loved the involvement of the professional game as it was in those days. He was a player at heart and was at home on the bus travelling to away games or in the bar after the match and he was terrific company. His clarion call was to the bus driver 'Driver, please stop at the nearest off licence so we can get some sherry for medicinal purposes' and in he would rush and come out with arms full of bottles of sherry. 'It settles the nerves.' Ronnie used to say and the amount he shifted must have left him with no nerves at all!

There always was a bottle of sherry for the players in our dressing room. He was and is my good friend (when he is sober), Ronnie Dobson.

BILL BOARDALL

This gentleman was one of the old school. He looked like everyone's favourite uncle. A typical Yorkshireman who never lost his native Halifax dialect, but a powerful man financially who hailed from a family of mill owners who were very 'well heeled' indeed.

Short in height but stockily built, Mr Boardall's pet love was the Yorkshire Senior Competition, the old A team league in his county. For years he was on the committee of that league and was a true believer of youth being prepared for the first team through the Senior Competition. A witty, dry comedian, Mr Boardall used to stand at the top of the old ramp that the players entered the field from on training nights and pass ribald comments on their fitness, waistline or lack of speed – not in a derogatory way, more a case of taking the mickey.

Our old mate Terry Dewhirst was on one of his many come-backs and doing his usual 40-odd laps of Thrum Hall, when Mr Boardall, who had been stood watching big Terry ploughing round the pitch, helped Terry make his mind up to retire for good when he called out to the big prop as he passed, 'Terry, don't tha think it's abart time tha packed it in?' and he did, because Mr Boardall was correct in his judgement.

When I arrived at Thrum Hall it was as a Wyatt Earp character, intent on 'cleaning up' the club. So much had to be done, not only the results on Sundays, but the whole persona of the club had to be picked up and shaken out of its lethargy. It needed a Joe Bastard and I was that Joe! Non-players were training with the squad and referees were coming and going at will and dictating training policy as there was no-one at the club with any ambition or knowledge of what to do or where to start to make it correct. If Mr Nice Guy had gone in he would have been swallowed without trace.

On my first night in charge I was challenged twice, by two non-players, and being much younger and fitter then, told them to leave or I would throw them out! One, a former referee, went to Bill Boardall and expecting things to be as they had been, said, 'Bill, the new coach has just threatened to throw me out of the ground if I don't go, what are we going to do about him?' Bill Boardall sucked on that old pipe of his, thought for a second or two then said 'If I were thee, I'd go now!'

Bill's other great love was the Halifax club itself. I did a bit of work at the club being a joiner by trade and I was finishing a job one day when in walked Bill. 'Will tha come into the boardroom, I want thee to look at a little job in there?' I went with Bill and there in the boardroom was this huge antique sideboard, with two large doors in the front.

'Can tha fix us a lock on this cupboard door?' he asked. I inspected the door and said I could and Bill continued, getting slowly down on his knees to reach into the very back of the old sideboard, 'Tha sees, somebody is getting into this cupboard and pinchin' these' and he drew out a teacup of the thick glazed pottery, in Blue and White hoops and the Halifax club coat of arms on the side. A real collector's item. Bill continued, 'When I used to come in here wi' me dad, this cupboard wor' full o' these cups and saucers, now tha's only one left. Somebody's nickin' 'em'. Bill was well turned 80 then and I couldn't bring myself to suggest natural breakages because of their age, but I put him a lock on his beloved sideboard and he was a happy favourite uncle. As I said, one of the old school, a nice man.

ANONYMOUS
The director who loved to dress up in his wife's underwear who, thinking it was his missus at the door, answered the bell in her attire and found me waiting, oops! and the director who, instead of planting the dummy plastic owl on the centre spot on the field to scare away the millions of starlings, was seen and heard throwing the plastic owl at them in an effort to frighten them away. Hello anyone at home?

13

REFEREES

PETER MASSEY

We hate 'em, we loathe 'em, we stick pins in their effigies but if we didn't have 'em there would be no game! Referees.

In the modern era the referee has taken a higher profile in the game and one or two because of TV exposure, have become stars, whereas in the olden days the players were the celebrities! People think of the excellent Fred Lindop as being the first pin-up boy of the refereeing fraternity but I recall my father telling me about the Reverend Frank Chambers who was as well-known as the players of his time.

I played under some good referees, Charlie Appleton (Warrington), 'Sergeant Major' Eric Clay (Rothwell), Mr TW Watkinson (Manchester), Matt Coats (Pudsey), Ron Gelder (Leeds), Mr RL 'Dicky' Thomas (Oldham), George Philpott (Leeds), Mr NT Railton (Wigan), Peter Gerraty (York) and many more, but it was in coaching that I got to know blokes like Stan Wall (Leigh), Mick Naughton (Widnes), Vince Moss and Peter Massey (both of Manchester), the one and only Billy Thompson (Huddersfield), Harry Hunt and Sam Shepherd (both from Lancashire) and Colin Morris, a St Helens lad, but registered out of Huddersfield. There are many tales about each but one such story involves Peter Massey.

I was coaching at Halifax and we were going well. We had a game at Keighley on a mid-winter Sunday afternoon; it had been freezing all the night before, but the sun came up early morning and there was an outside chance that the game would go ahead. Keighley were having a good run too, under coach Alan Kellett, and I was just a little worried that it was the wrong time for us to be playing them, particularly at Lawkholme Lane, as we had one or two injuries to contend with.

We arrived at the ground about 2:00pm for a 3:00pm kick off and had a look at the pitch straight away. Peter Massey was already out on the field checking on the playing area. At 2:00pm the centre of the pitch was just about playable but an area about 3 feet inside the field of play from the touchline, down the full length of the field had been in the shadow of the low stand at the ground all morning and was rock hard. Mr Massey asked, as I dug my heel in the half frozen centre spot, 'What do you think Maurice?'

'It's too hard, Peter' I said, 'and it will harden up towards half-time and will be dangerous for the players in the second half when the sun has gone and the frost sets in.'

Peter walked around and looked at the strip of frozen ground under the stand. 'I agree, match off' said the referee.

Now the Keighley chairman wanted the match on. He had rather foolishly opened the turnstiles and a fairly big crowd had come into the ground and were filling up both stands. 'Come on' said the home chairman, 'it's playable. I've seen games played on worse than this.'

But Peter was adamant, 'Sorry, it's off' he said.

'Look, I'll have the touchline marked out 3 feet infield, to clear the frozen part,' the chairman said.

Now things had gone my way up to now, I didn't want to play the game but this latest suggestion from the chairman put a bit of doubt in Peter's mind. 'Would that be OK with you?' Peter asked me.

'Only if he moves both sets of goal posts 18 inches to give an even distance from the touchlines,' I said, hoping that this would be an end to the business.

'Match off' said the ref and away he went back to Manchester. The admission fee was £1 and amid calling us all sorts of names, the chairman had two of his staff, with hands full of £1 notes, giving each spectator their money back as they shuffled out of the ground. Ronnie Dobson and I had a £1 note thrust into our hands as we left too, but we both paid to get in when we came back and won later in the season.

STAN WALL

Stan was a cracking little referee. He retired at the maximum age for referees and went onto the backroom staff at St Helens RLFC in the kit room, and can still be seen carrying on the kicking tee when Saints are on TV. Stan worked in the coal mining industry and, at the time of the terrible miners' strikes, was on the staff working in the office as well as being on the top of his game as a professional referee.

During these bad times, the miners on the picket lines would only allow into the pits workers and messengers who were looking after the safety of the mines so that work could continue once the strikes were over. Stan was at a pit in Leigh and was told to take some safety papers over to a particularly militant pit in Castleford. As Stan approached the Yorkshire pit the pickets saw the NCB van which Stan was driving and immediately attacked it. The vehicle was shook violently and the pickets tried to pull Stan out of the van, with shouts of 'Get him out' and 'String him up'.

Stan was scared and called out, 'Hold it lads; I'm only delivering some safety papers'.

The pickets continued rocking the van and one leader shouted out, 'We're not bothered about the bloody papers, that's Stan Wall the referee in this van and he robbed Castleford last week when we lost to Wigan. Get him out and string him up!'

Luckily Stan was saved by the police and snuck back to Lancashire unscathed. A grand referee was Stan!

BILLY THOMPSON

A wonderful referee, superb after-dinner speaker and a nice bloke is Billy. He tells a tale about refereeing a tough cup tie at Widnes when Jim Mills was in his pomp and knocking players sideways with his all-out action game. Play went up-field and Billy saw out of the corner of his eye big Jim and an opposition forward having a tussle. When he looked again Jim was stood up and the forward was laid out. 'Billy,' said Jim, 'you won't believe me but I never touched him'.

Billy weighed it up and said, 'Look Jim, there's only you, me and him anywhere near here and I didn't hit him, so off you go lad' and promptly sent him off.

Billy used to train with us at Fartown when I coached Huddersfield and I used to put him through it to some tune, but to his credit he stuck to his guns and was never a quitter. I have often wondered if it was our good training that made him a top referee!

Another wise guy tried it on with Billy; he made a nuisance of himself and tried to spoil a good open game. Billy warned and penalised him several times until he could take no further insults to his refereeing. Now Billy knew the player very well and indeed had known him for years, but he was forced to go through the procedure of sending him off by the book!

'Come here number 12' Billy called, pulling out the dreaded sending-off book and pencil. The forward trudged over to Billy with a smirk on his face, 'Name' said Billy.

'You know my name' the sarcastic player answered.

'Name,' Billy repeated, 'and you know the drill as well as me, now, name'.

The player waited an age then said, with another smirk, 'Mickey Mouse'.

Billy looked up from his book, a slight smile on his lips and said, 'Right off you go Mickey' and the forward turned away with a sour face, never thinking his old mate would walk him, then as he was about five yards away, Billy called after him, 'And Mickey, give my regards to Minnie!'

A foible Billy had in common with Stan Wall, was that on occasions he would, at the second the ball was played and he had given the five yards onside, shuffle back 18 inches, thus calling the defensive side offside. I remember as coach at Wigan once coming off the field and talking about this habit with Billy, 'Do you realise you are doing it Billy?' I asked.

'Oh yes, I know that I do it, irritating isn't it!' and he disappeared into the referees' room.

As he got older, like most of us, he struggled to keep that bit too much weight off, and I know that if he ever reads this he will deny it. But a fit Billy Thompson was a terrific referee and even as a rotund whistle blower he was a top man.

14

THE WRITERS

JOE HUMPHREYS

Some of the greatest characters in the game have been the writers who bring, week after week, the news of matches from around the leagues. When the tours to Australia and New Zealand were on a regular four-year cycle, the same reporting journalists went tour after tour, and firm and lasting friendships were made between players and writers. Of course those with long memories will remember Eddie Waring, Jack Bentley, Alan Cave, Jack McNamarra and Joe Humphreys. In later years we were entertained by the facts from Peter Wilson, John Huxley, Brian Battey, Martin Richards, Ian Laybourne, David Hadfield, Trevor Watson and many other fine rugby league writers.

On tour many tricks were played on the young, first-time tourist fledgling writers by the case-hardened, experienced touring players. One favourite trick by the players if the writer was staying at the same hotel, was to gain the room number of a 'rookie' journalist and order drinks and meals on his bill, paid for of course by the wealthy newspaper.

The 1950 tourists were the last to go by sea, and it was then a five to six week journey on the 'briny' with stops at exotic ports and some not so exotic! At one of the latter in the Gulf area, there was a full blooded war going on when the liner docked. The tourists arrived safely in their overnight hotel as the sound of gunfire came nearer and nearer. One of the old school writers, Joe Humphreys of the *Daily Mirror*, a gentleman to his boot tops, wanted to get his copy back to the office in Manchester and in all his years as a top journalist had never been late and he was not going to start now!

No phone lines working in the hotel, the liner temporarily out of bounds, and every public phone out of order, Joe was in a fix! So he set off walking through the town, saw a public phone, and on trying it, lo and behold, it worked!

As Joe dialled the newspaper's Manchester number, he looked out of the phone box and saw a huge Sherman tank swing in to the road that he was in phoning home. This phone was the last link with civilisation as he knew it and Joe was spelling out his copy to the desk for the next morning paper amid the banging of mortars and the rumbling of tanks passing only feet away.

Suddenly a BBC war correspondent attempted to snatch the handset away from our intrepid *Daily Mirror* man, with the verbal tongue lashing of 'Don't hog the phone, don't you know there's a war on?'

Our rugby league writer coolly finished his report with, 'But Alex Murphy should be fit for the first game in Darwin,' rang off and turned to the war correspondent and said, 'That was far more important than war news. That was the Rugby League Lions Tour news'.

As always, that great journalist Joe Humphreys had his priorities right!

TREVOR WATSON

Of course our games writers covered everything going on in the season, not just tours, and one of the most enjoyable tasks was to cover the Wembley progress of the local team and should the team go all the way, then it was a pleasant trip indeed to the then twin towers!

Trevor Watson reported on the Leeds club for many,

many years and covered a few Wembleys in his time and on one trip he recalls an unusual encounter with a newfangled camera!

Leeds had played well getting into the final and Trevor had been invited to travel with the team and stay at the same hotel. This gave Trevor the chance to send his reports back to his paper, the *Yorkshire Evening Post*, to let the team's supporters know how things were shaping up in the final few days to the big game. International second rower, Phil Cookson was keen to capture as much of the once in a lifetime experience on film as he could and as Trevor accompanied the team on their pre-match walk around 'God's Green Acre', Phil produced this ultra-expensive brand new camera and, as Trevor was from the newspaper industry, he expected the reporter to be a second 'Lord Lichfield' so asked him to do the honours.

Trevor checked with Phil as to the workings of this wondrous machine, grouped the Leeds team together, all happy and smiling, expecting this snap to be entered in the *Photo of the Year competition*. Click, click, click, Trevor fired off a trio of shots, marvelling at the speed of the automatic shutter, and was fancying his chances as the photographer of the century when he was brought back down to earth by Phil Cookson calling to him, 'Trevor, you've got the f****** thing the wrong way round'.

On retrieving the film from the chemists, there they were three cracking pictures of Trevor's eyes and nose. Trevor Watson was, and is, one of the game's most knowledgeable and honest writers, but photographer, hmm!

ANONYMOUS

It would be unfair of me to name the journalist from this tale as he received the mother and father of telling offs for printing this story with names included as the local newspaper it appeared in covered the Bramley club. It centres on the Bramley coach at the time, the former Great Britain, Castleford, Leeds and Hull FC half-back, Keith Hepworth.

The club had signed two of my former players, Malcolm Branch and Graham Swales from Huddersfield and 'Heppy' was expecting great things from them. 'Swazzer' Swales was a notorious prankster who hated training and all things appertaining to getting fit! He could play mark you, but the training part of the game didn't interest him.

This particular night was cold and with the ground frozen over, Heppy decided to send the players on a road run. The usual procedure on these runs was that the coach mapped out the route, sent the squad off and followed at a discreet distance in his car, usually with his assistant riding shotgun, to check that all was in order. As Swazzer passed Heppy, the coach heard the jingle of money in his pocket, and knowing that it wouldn't be the first time that certain players had caught the bus to cover the route, he demanded to know what was jingling!

'My car keys Keith' said Swazzer and both players, Branch and Swales were allowed to continue on the run. Ten minutes later Heppy and his assistant drove slowly along the designated route and as they approached *Harrison's Fish and Chip Emporium*, two figures were seen huddled together tucking into newspaper-covered, 'once and a fish'. It was Branchy and Swazzer. In for seconds they went, with Heppy watching every move, then after their feast, went to the bus shelter to wait for the next public transport that went passed the ground on Bramley Town Street.

Keith Hepworth never said a word to them, he just dropped them from the first team and when the irate players asked 'Why are we dropped?' Heppy said, 'Because of suspected food poisoning!'

Could it happen today? I think not, but even at the time these things were happening – which were few and far between may I add – they were never talked about, hence the telling off of the writer by his boss.

THE MEDIA AND GREAT BRITAIN

Was my face red one day in the Great Britain camp at Lilleshall! In preparation for the 1986 Aussie Tests we took the squad to the National Sports Centre for a week's coaching. We got through all of our skills work, played out our defensive drills and really worked hard ensuring we were ready for the Tests.

The squad needed a change from hard work, something to lighten the load. The press were due to visit us in camp on the Thursday afternoon but phoned through to say it would be cancelled. We had prepared a skills display that would knock their eyes out, all to no avail. So, as we had a spare session in private we decided to give the lads a free and easy 'soft' session in competition, but having things like egg and spoon races and sack races, all the things to have a laugh with.

Everything was going great guns, peals of laughter ringing from the squad, everyone having a real good time and we were half way through the wheelbarrow race with the barrow holding a spoon with an egg in it in his mouth, whilst being pushed by the legs, when we noticed an army of sour-faced pressmen and newspaper writers stood lined up at the side of the field, watching in disbelief. I heard one say, 'And this is how we will beat the Aussies!' No, it is what you call having a bit of fun, the hard work was done but it was just bad timing.

Les Bettinson, my manager, explained the reason for the frivolity and it was accepted by the writers, but was my face red? I'll say!

15

CHARACTERS IN THE AMATEUR GAME

THE DOWLING BROTHERS, KEIRON DEAKIN AND MANY MORE

Before Super League and the days of each club developing its own players at junior level, the way into professional rugby league was via the amateur leagues, either the junior leagues or be seen and signed on through the open age competitions.

Throughout the counties of Yorkshire, Lancashire and Cumberland (as it was then) hundreds of amateur clubs existed before BARLA, in and around the big cities and small villages. They were run from big factories and one-man firms, from schools' old boys' associations and corner public houses.

The first organised league team I played for was a very old club, Burley Vale, and this little club was run from the secretary's scullery in a back-to-back house on Hyde Park Road, Leeds.

Amateur clubs could be found in the grounds of some better-off professional teams, at Youth Clubs, on council estates and even formed within a young player's home where a group of mates had banded together and one of the dads had contacted the local league to gain admission.

There were many different amateur leagues in the three counties because of the number of teams that wanted to play the game. And in some areas a number of good sides sought out membership of more competitive leagues in other towns and cities as they were just too strong in their own area.

Such was the case with the ultra successful Dewsbury Celtic, who although maintaining a paid up membership of the Heavy Woollen League, played all their matches in the old, very strong, Leeds and District League. And the tremendous Brookhouse side from Wakefield joined the Leeds and District, to get the highly competitive fixtures that this grand team needed to maintain its power. Lock Lane from Castleford too played for many years in the same league and were a fearsome outfit, but the local teams within the City of Leeds were generally strong sides.

Buslingthorpe Vale played at the locally known pitch, Bus Vale, in the valley of Meanwood, at the bottom of the historic Woodhouse Ridge, a steep wooded hillside opposite Sugerwell hill where in the Civil War, the Cavaliers had a set-to with the Roundheads but even they could not match the battles of Bus Vale, where even today, most of the league's finals take place.

It was at Bus Vale each close season that the annual Workshops Competition was played, when companies in Leeds would form a team, from ex-amateur and former professional players and be allowed three 'permit' players, men who were playing for bona fide amateur clubs and usually two professionals who would be on a pro clubs books. Needless to say there was a heck of a lot of fiddling took place and some big money bets were made on the eventual winners of this highly entertaining knockout competition.

The winning team's players would each be presented with a canteen of cutlery, or a weather barometer, for the hallway at home or some traditional prize for winning the Workshops. These money-making knockouts were also held at the professional grounds and very big crowds attended

Bus Vale, Headingley and Parkside on summer evenings, to watch all the various rounds, right through to the final. Several businessmen around the city with experience in the amateur game would get together some good sides and pay the professionals (and some of the better amateurs) then make up their outlay by having a good bet on the final. Walter Rooks, a local greengrocer in Woodhouse, ran a team for years in the Bus Vale Workshops and always looked after his better players.

There were quite a few talent scouts from the professional clubs at these games too and many a good lad has gone on to better things by playing in the Workshops. One can imagine how much money was generated from the gate alone, with full houses at a lot of the games especially local derbies or where two teams were well fancied. The old Bus Vale club used to run the knockouts and would cover all the club's expenses for the coming season on the ticket receipts.

When the Bus Vale club disbanded, the Rugby Football League bought the old place and leased it out to the Leeds and District League, who for a short while ran the knockouts to help finance the District League.

Some good times were had, and some great matches seen in the days of the Workshops at Bus Vale!

Another fantastic competition that has run for many years is the superb 'Champion of Champions', an invitation competition that was the brainchild of the Leigh Miners Welfare Club. The excellent ground at the Welfare, situated behind the clubhouse is the perfect setting for this magnificent and elite competition. Only the champions of the top leagues around the country are invited to join this festival of wonderful entertaining rugby league football and so popular was this close season competition that the draw for the various rounds was, at one time, made on *Radio*

Manchester and the local BBC regional TV!

One can't mention the great Leigh Miners Welfare Club without spending a moment remembering the wonderful service this old-established club has done for the game both at amateur level and for its endless production line producing top professional players over many years. Two of the club's better known sons are the famous brothers, Paul and Robert Dowling, who when younger, would sooner have a fight than their dinner! Two terrific players, tough, brave and skilful, they strode the North West Counties like giants for many seasons, playing purely for the love of the game.

I remember only too well, I was coach of the professional club, Halifax, being drawn to play the courageous Miners Welfare, at Hilton Park, the then name of Leigh RLFC, in the John Player Trophy in 1978. In a tight struggle we managed to win and being the professional team, I took a collection of £5 per man on our bus and offered it to the Dowling brothers as a gift from us.

'Nay lad' Robert said, 'We have more money at the Welfare than you do at Halifax. Thanks very much but no, we can't accept it'. No hard feelings, I went out the following week and purchased a lovely big trophy, had it suitably inscribed and we presented it to the Miners Welfare committee a few weeks later. To my knowledge it is still in the Welfare's trophy cabinet.

But of all the fine competitions run, the finest, for both professionals and amateurs, is the Rugby League Challenge Cup. In the old days before BARLA, amateur sides throughout the counties would embark in the competition to reach the first round proper. Only two teams went through in those days, one from the knockout rounds in Yorkshire and one similar in a joint competition held in Lancashire and Cumbria. The amateur stage was known as the qualifying rounds and the final two teams went into the draw with the big boys.

If a club went through not only was it a great pay day but the side that played in the first round proper went down in the club's folklore history, and even today teams that went through years ago are spoken of in awe. Speaking only of the 'old days', and not of the recent great deeds by such as West Hull, Oldham St Anne's, Woolston Rangers and Sharlston Rovers who can boast victories over professional sides in the Challenge Cup as it stands today, there were several amateur sides that gained wins over their more illustrious opponents. In 1905–06 the redoubtable coal miners from Featherstone Rovers beat Widnes, 23 points to 2 in round two of the cup, two years later Whitehaven Recreation beat St Helens by 13 points to 8 and in 1908–09 Beverley created a shock when they beat the strong Ebbw Vale by 7 points to 2.

Later the first round became a two-legged affair and, in 1945–46, the forerunner of todays Sharlston Rovers, Sharlston Red Rose won the home leg, 12 points to 7 against Workington Town, only to go out of the cup being beaten 16 points to 2 in the second leg in Cumbria. The very gallant Risehow and Gillhead lost in the first leg at Keighley, in 1947–48, by 11 points to nil but in a valiant effort in Cumbria, won the second leg by 10 points to 2, but lost overall on aggregate. Deeds of glory, indeed.

In 1960 the Barrow based amateur side, Walney Central and Lock Lane from Castleford won through to the first round proper and against all the odds, were drawn against each other in a fantastic all-amateur game. In a pulsating clash, Walney Central won by ten points to five. Then a strange occurrence in 1964 saw Thames Board Mills go through to round two because Bradford Northern disbanded only to be beaten in the next stage by 48 points to 8 at Blackpool Borough.

Many other amateur teams earned their 80 minutes of

glory by fighting their way into the hat for the Challenge Cup draw. The club that gave me my first chance as a coach, Stanningley, went to the first round proper twice. The first time was in the mid 1950s, against Rochdale Hornets when all the advice from local teams who had been through into the 'big time' was that the amateurs would get no ball from the set scrums as the professionals would be too big and have too much know-how and the Stanningley boys would be chasing and tackling all afternoon. So they concentrated all their efforts into a defensive programme, ignoring any attacking policy, went to the old Athletic Ground at Rochdale and won almost every scrum. In fact they had so much ball, they didn't know what to do with it!

A defeat by 20 odd points was not a tragic one but the players felt that with a little better advice they may have done even better. But what may well have happened is that the old-headed professionals may have outsmarted the amateurs with a ploy that was used regularly in Test football. The ploy was to let the team have the ball, not attempting to win the ball from the scrum and even kicking to them from the kick-off. And remembering that the game then was played under unlimited tackles, you knocked hell out of them for as long as it took to 'soften them up!' It was a ploy used by our international team against, more often than not, the French, who were thought to be brittle against hard tackling. And just maybe that's why Stanningley won so much ball!

The mastermind behind this Stanningley side that came from nowhere to become the premier team in the ultra tough Leeds and District was the late Harry Moore, who as manager, chairman, coach and main man for many years started the successful ball rolling by changing the club's name and giving the team a new identity by buying the first set of playing kit himself.

Formerly the Wagon and Horses, a pub team that changed in the establishment's cellar, Harry Moore had the foresight to call the club after the area in which it played – Stanningley. He visualised a strong, tough side that would need a tough, no nonsense style strip! He ordered a black jersey with a white V, brought in new players to bolster the good nucleus of existing ones and from there, success bred success as the team gained the Leeds League Trophy then the Yorkshire Open Age Cup was lifted at the old Barley Mow ground, and qualification into the first round proper of the Challenge Cup.

The second Challenge Cup appearance was in the mid-1960s, again with a very tough and physical team, and again the tactics were not quite right and this cracking amateur side slid to a heavy defeat against a very special cup-fighting team, Featherstone Rovers.

As a youngster I remember a pub team from St Helens, the Vine Tavern, playing tremendously well in a cup-tie at the old Barley Mow ground against Bramley and beating the home professional side, in fact looking likely to beat them altogether until, in a game played in very stormy conditions, a set of the posts blew down causing the match to be abandoned with the amateurs in the lead.

Teams from the Warrington district always went well in the qualifying rounds, Latchford Albion, Rylands Recs and Crossfields could be relied on to do well and moving towards 'the hill' Saddleworth, Langworthy Juniors and the wonderfully traditional Oldham St Anne's took some beating. The big cup in the Oldam area was the superb Standard Cup. The final was at the old Watersheddings ground and played each Good Friday morning with an 11:00am kick off. What a scene with over 4,000 spectators, an atmosphere that could be cut with a knife and fierce rivalry between whoever were the finalists. As an amateur coach I linked up with the St

Anne's club and spent many a happy Good Friday in the cracking company of the 'Anne's' lads, who proudly claimed the title of the 'Mighty Green and Golds' and the superb singing group lead by the man himself, Bernard Richardson, was a delight to hear as the ale flowed making drinking afternoons as good as footballing mornings.

Over the years I brought a few players into professional football from both St Anne's and their local rivals, Waterhead. One forward with everything going for him I took from St Anne's was Keiron Deakin, a big, strong, fast second rower from a famous Oldham rugby league family where all the brothers followed dad Peter Deakin into the game. A dear pal of mine, the late and sadly missed Peter was a good player himself but became better known for his work in marketing the game and did excellent work both for Bradford Bulls and Warrington Wolves as well as in the Rugby Union field at Sale and in London at Saracens. Stephen has done well in the coaching world and Chris has worked wonders with the St Anne's club as coach after a long career as a tough forward mainly at Rochdale Hornets. Michael played professionally at Prescot, and of course there was Keiron.

After a while Keiron wanted to be back with his family and mates in amateur football but instead of coming to me and talking about it, he just went missing. Try as I might, I couldn't find neither hide nor hair of him so, as a last resort I contacted Roger Halstead at the *Oldham Chronicle* and ask him to run a 'Wanted Dead or Alive' advert in the newspaper. It read, in large print on the sports page of the 'Chron' *Wanted Dead or Alive, knowledge of the whereabouts of Keiron Deakin. The Dewsbury club offer a substantial reward for his capture and safe return to Crown Flatts. Contact Maurice Bamford at the club office.*

Roger ran the ad free of charge and Keiron contacted me;

we had a good talk and a laugh about the ad, sorted out his problems, then he told me that the page in the Chron with the advert had been enlarged and put on the wall of St Anne's then headquarters, the Spotted Cow pub in Oldham.

A great set of lads and St Anne's headquarters now are a credit to all the hard workers at the club who rebuilt the original clubhouse after a fire gutted the superb building. When I was a regular visitor the posse included the Deakin mob, Joe Leach, Alan Taylor, Billy Heron, Bernard Richardson and a host more who are truly rugby league men.

In the days of which we speak, one did not travel far from one's own environment so my involvement with the amateur game was around the Leeds area and again because of the only movement from your own neck of the woods was if you were drawn away in the Yorkshire Cup, there was no Pennine League or National Conference, no playing in another town, let alone another county. The exception to that was, as I explained earlier, teams like Dewsbury Celtic, Brookhouse and Lock Lane, playing outside their own areas. There were three clubs from York played in the Leeds and District: York Imperial, Heworth and Southlands and one from the area between Dewsury and Wakefield, Ossett Trinity. There was a nice little team from Thorpe – a village which became the sprawling Middleton Estate – Bison Sports, Burton Sports, Stanningley and Kirkstall Forge and going a shade further back, Buslingthorpe Vale.

I signed as an amateur for the Leeds club but at 17 years old signed as a professional for Hull FC, then still playing at The Boulevard. Leeds refused me permission to train with the amateur junior team I had played for so I had to train at the nearest amateur club once a week which was Bus Vale. When I trained there the club was a strong one with many players well known in the Leeds area. One of the best known was Jackie Brown, a prop forward who had represented England amateurs in the first international match after the Second World War. Jackie was immensely strong and superbly built for a prop. He was quick too with a fine burst of speed and was a crunching tackler. He was an athlete too, his party trick on leaving the communal bath in the dressing room was to perform a perfect hand stand on the end of the solid rubbing down table and with the glistening muscled body in perfect line with extended arms, proceed to do slight dips from the elbow until his head touched the table, then straightened out the elbows again. And this he did several times!

Jackie Brown was also a war hero. I met him in 1953 only a short eight years after the war had ended when he would have been in his early 30s. He never once mentioned his heroism but it was quietly known that he was awarded the top French military medal for bravery in saving French soldiers in one action, and he was a nice man too.

Billy Russell was a wingman with county and international experience. Small in stature Billy made up for this with pace and aggression. He was a big mate of Jackie Brown and a most likeable bloke. I remember Billy when I was a kid and I used to see him now and again when we helped out at Headingley on Saturday mornings to clear the snow from the playing field. Billy worked at that time for Sir Edwin Airey, the builder who was also the chairman of the Leeds club, and Billy was in charge of 'snow-shifting' but the other kids who knew him used to say that he was a good player.

As I was growing up I found out myself that he was just that. I coached his youngest son, John, at Dewsbury and he too was a cracking little player. Billy was also at Bus Vale when I trained there, as was the third of the trio of mates, Ron Sellers, a hooker and along with Jackie and Billy formed the inseparable 'Three Musketeers'.

The tough derby games in West Leeds were the fixture trio of Stanningley, Hawksworth Old Boys and Leeds Electric. Rich characters indeed as these warriors had returned either from the 1939–45 war, or were fresh back from National Service. Leeds Electric, 'The Lights' as they were nicknamed, boasted two tremendous props, Harold Price and Percy Isaacs, with a classical scrum half and loose forward pairing of Lennie Patricks and Charlie Kenny. Whilst Hawksworth Old Boys, a club founded on the Hawksworth Estate in North West Leeds, produced a hard, uncompromising outfit which included, in their pack, brothers Geoff and Louis Smith, Clarrie Briggs, who later had several good seasons playing at the Batley club, the enthusiastic and wonderful Harold Oddy, ex Leeds and Castleford professional who played in the Sunday league until well into his fifties, the scheming Jimmy Keeble at half-back and Bob Dawson at loose forward. Grand players all, and tough.

Across the River Aire from Hawksworth was the Bramley and Stanningley areas of Leeds. Stanningley were the premier side for a few years and had a successful run assisted by Colin Bird, Ronnie Swales, Eric Joyce, Billy Slater, Steve Hey, Phil Harrison, Ronnie Stead, Al Dickinson, Freddy Dean, Fred Nugent and many more. In later seasons the side boasted John Cave, Jeff Bell, Len Thompson, Trevor Elliott, Leon Harrison, Jack Shaw, Harold Oddy and Keith Norman, the latter two coming from the Hawksworth club.

So many great amateur players were around in those days, many I have not mentioned, but across the City there were two teams who gave everyone a hard game, Middleton Old boys and Middleton Colliery. The Old Boys had a superb pair in Wardle and Dawson, whilst the Colliery had two fearless props in Charlie Mann and his big mate, Ray Coleman. At scrum half was a man who was like another forward, Colin Morton. Again both Middleton sides had many great players, and the local professional clubs knew where to look should they require a tough player for any position – up at 'Miggy'.

The amateur game in the pre Super League days was seen as essential in producing adult players as well as juniors. A great many amateurs took the professional ticket at an age that today would be classed as too old!

Obviously the method of today's recruitment into the professional game helps the amateur clubs in that they can usually keep their open age players for longer periods than before when the pro clubs would accept players at a much older age. The players now are taken under the professional wing much younger with the successful professional academy setup and players as young as 12, 13 and 14 years of age being given the type of professional coaching and fitness programmes that would have been frowned upon some years ago.

Heavy intensity because of the increased financial inducements seems to have replaced the 'Play for the sake of playing' attitude that was prevalent in days gone by, but on the good side, the players coming back from the Pro game should be more skilful and have good fitness habits. That is if they do come back to the amateur game, as recent statistics show quite a lot are leaving the game if they fail in the professional big time, which is a crying shame.

Many players too turned to refereeing when the day came to hang up their playing boots. Laurie Gant, the guru of the old National Coaching Scheme, who played at Wembley for Featherstone Rovers in 1952 and coached the same team to victory at the twin towers in 1967, was also an international referee. The brothers George and Alan Thorpe from Leeds officiated for years after ending their playing days, as did an old team mate of mine, Geoff Clarke, from our Burton Sports years. The other Geoff Clarke, brother of my old hooker Peter, the referee that Peter 'told his dad about' back in chapter 8, was a professional player too and he had many happy seasons blowing his whistle! Bernard Robinson was a pro player who refereed for many years and worked hard for the amateur game and in the recruitment of young officials.

Bernard was the referee who sent me off in my last ever game as a player when, as coach at Stanningley I took my team to play the strong Heworth side, away, and were one man short so I subbed and had to go on in the dying moments. My entry coincided with a scrum and the young prop opposite me tested me with his 'nut' first time up. Mr Robinson called us out and warned us. We went to the scrum again and the kid was at it once more, so I gave him a clout and was dismissed by the excellent Mr Robinson (although he was wrong on this occasion). And, by the way, the young prop who fancied himself that day later in his career captained Great Britain for me – Hull Kingston Rover's David Watkinson.

Another good referee was a team mate of mine as a player at Stanningley, Ray Duckworth. A true tale this, Ray was subbing for us in a Yorkshire Cup tie at the ultra tough ground of the famous Siddal amateur club in Halifax. Unbeaten for a few years on their own pitch the enormity of the task was brought home to us on a windy and rain drenched Saturday afternoon when we saw the field ankle deep in mud and with a slope steeper than the Mount Pleasant ground at Batley. As a sub, Ray was in charge of the 'money bag', a small canvas bag into which all the players placed their money, watches, rings, car keys and anything of value, for safe keeping.

Our experienced side were at the top of our game that afternoon and 20 minutes from time held an unassailable lead by around twenty clear points. I had managed to sneak in at the corner – after a run of at least two yards – to put the result beyond doubt and as the team's goal kicker, had the dubious task of converting my own try into the teeth of the gale, on a very muddy pitch, in the pouring rain, with a fairly big crowd baying for my blood!

As a 'toe ender' I carefully paced out my run, and all the time I could hear Ray Duckworth's voice calling, 'Come on then, put your money where your mouth is. He will blow this over; any more of you mugs want to bet?' Concentrating very hard on the kick and taking one final look at the posts, which seemed a million miles away, I waited for a lull in the gale and seizing my chance, hit as sweet a kick as I ever did. Bang! Straight between those posts and over the crossbar.

We won by a good 30 points at the end and as we walked to the dressing rooms, Ray came to me, smiling, and said, 'Thanks Maurice, you got me out of trouble there. I had over £100 on that goal kick and the wager was all out of the money bag'. The lads had a free nights boozing on Ray's profits, but had I missed that difficult goal kick it would have been a different outcome for Ray Duckworth!

Referees act as touch judges too and a mate of mine was running the line in a Yorkshire Cup Final for a well-known referee of the time. My mate saw an infringement and went on the field; flag raised, and reported it.

As he was marking the 10 yards back, the forward he had reported called him a few choice names as he past him, so on he went again and the referee awarded another penalty and warned the player about his future conduct. Again the player verbally abused my mate so on he went again. By this time the crowd were cat-calling my mate and wanted to see some playing action. The referee, a Lancastrian, told my mate, 'I can't send him off, it's the county cup final,' so he warned the player again and back they went another ten yards.

Sensing he was 'untouchable' the player again swore at my mate as he passed and that was the final straw. My mate put his flag on the ground and walked onto the field. The referee ran over to him and my mate said, 'That's three times he has verbally abused me. Now either he walks, or I do. The flag is there, it's up to you'.

The referee did the right thing, he walked the player!

16

THEY SAID IT

PETER FOX

Since the game of rugby football began words, intended to be of wisdom, have occasionally come out all wrong or the speaker has left an indelible mark on the folklore of the game, because of what they said. I have mentioned the 'noose' in France, back in chapter 12 and how I learned a lesson there, but there have been many other tales handed down which enhance the humour of the speaker and should be saved for posterity.

The great coach and long-serving player in the game, Peter Fox, is mistakenly not noted as such a great player although Peter had many seasons as a regular first team player at Batley, Hull KR, and Featherstone Rovers, but because of the exceptional ability of his two international brothers, Don and Neil, Peter's playing abilities are often underrated. I have a different view as Peter knows the game inside out and his prowess as a coach stemmed from his great knowledge of the game. But it is the legacy of tales about Peter, and the mythical stories that abound about the guy, that make hilarious retelling time after time.

Peter is supposed to tell the story of the world-renowned hard forward and former professional boxer, Wigan's Brian McTigue, holder of twenty-five caps for Great Britain against all the top hard teams of his time. 'Hard?' Peter is reported to have said, 'Hard? McTigue only played against me once and after two scrums at prop, asked to be moved into the second row, I soon shifted him!' Now the word was that the only bloke who could shift McTigue at the time was Rocky Marciano, but those are the tales about Peter.

In a pre-match speech before a Batley v Wakefield Trinity game, Peter is supposed to have addressed his Batley team-mates and said, 'I'll take care of Rocky Turner and you other twelve can take care of our Neil!' And in another pre-match oratory when Batley were playing Featherstone Rovers, Peter is said to tell the Batley players, 'Featherstone will be easy today, they only have one good player and that's our Don!' Unfortunately Featherstone won by a cricket score.

Peter tells the story of his debut for Featherstone Rovers at Barrow when that doyen of stand-off halves, Willie Horne, was performing wonders for the 'Shipbuilders' at Craven Park. Peter's coach was the tremendous wingman, Eric Batten, who had toured with Willie on the 1946 trip, had played against him many times and knew of the fabulous Barrow player's abilities. 'Get to him early Peter and don't leave him all afternoon; wherever Willie Horne goes, you go, and knock him down every time!' Peter says that the only time he touched Willie Horne was when the final whistle ended the game and he shook hands with him!

Say what you want about Peter Fox, he was and is a character of our game and my dad used to say that people only talk about you if you are a good 'un. I agree!

FRANK 'SHANKS' WATSON

Once again we delve into the folklore of the old Hunslet club and a tale related to me about that great footballer, the former Hunslet and Leeds half-back, Frank Watson. Frank – 'Shanks' to all at the time he played with – was a player of wonderful skills, a 'feeder' of superbly timed passes that had runners ploughing into gaps wider than the 'Morley tunnel'. A copybook tackler and kicker and a superbly fast player of the ball after being tackled, Frank could do anything asked of him on a rugby league field, a champion player. The tale centres on the thinking of the then board of directors.

The story goes that Frank agreed to sign for Hunslet in August 1939 for a fee of £50. His money would be there to collect on the 3rd of September and Frank called into the club on the day to pick it up. The secretary handed Frank a pay packet and said, 'The board met this morning to authorise your payment of £50, but as war was declared today, they have decided to give you £10 now and the remainder at the end of the current hostilities'.

Another five years to wait for his forty quid and worth every penny! The great 'Shanks' Watson.

GORDON MURRAY

Gordon Murray was a director of the reborn New Hunslet club who played at the Greyhound Stadium opposite Elland Road, home of Leeds United AFC. In one early cup tie the New Hunslet team were drawn at home to a highly placed Lancashire side and the board at the 'Dog-Track' decided to offer a bonus for winning.

In those days the usual bonus in the early rounds was, say, a tenner per man. But Gordon, always a man to do a business deal, had another idea about the bonus and his announcement did not go down well when he proudly proclaimed that if the side won, the players would each receive a 'frozen chicken apiece'. The Lancashire team won easily and at first Gordon was determined that the team would not be given the bonus, but after realising that the chickens would not keep much longer out of the freezer, he relented and gave the players 'the bird'.

TOMMY GRAINEY

That great servant of the game, former Leigh utility-back and coach at various clubs, Tommy Grainey, was assistant coach to his old mate, Kevin Ashcroft at Salford, and things were up one week and down the next as the pair of very knowledgeable men attempted to get some sort of consistency into their results. A good win away from home was followed a week later by a sickening defeat at the Willows by a team they should have beaten comfortably. Kevin as senior coach was at his wits end and told Tommy it might be better if he went in the dressing room to speak to the team as if he, Kevin, went in he may well lose his temper and sack the lot of them. Tommy thought it was a good idea and set off for the changing area.

Now Tommy, on occasions, got his words mixed up and usually it ended up in laughing hysterics. The dressing room was like a cemetery when he arrived. Silent players sat with their heads in their hands, no-one speaking and generally everyone feeling terribly sorry for themselves. 'Come on lads,' Tommy pleaded, 'this is no good, feeling bloody sorry for yourselves. You've got to get up off the bloody floor like a good fighter. There is another match next week that hasn't been bloody touched yet and it gives you another chance to bloody put things right'.

Gradually the players began to come around, not because Tommy was giving them pearls of wisdom, but because he had never said as much without getting his words mixed up! They were waiting for a punch line. 'That's better lads,' Tommy said, feeling the lightness coming back into the room, 'after all, so we've lost a bloody match, it's not the end of the bloody MOON'. He had done it again, the dressing room erupted into fits of laughter, and that was Tommy's strong suit, the ability to 'bring a team back' as he has such good football sense and is such a nice bloke.

On a coaching seminar at a top Leeds hotel, Tommy had decided he had supped enough on the first night as the coaches relaxed in the hotel bar. Off he went to bed and about two hours later he reappeared, room keys in his hand and said to me, 'Morrish, I can't open my f****** bedroom door, give us a hand, old mate' and staggered off again towards the lift. I went up with him, checking that he had the correct floor, and as we approached his room, he passed his door and went to the door further on the corridor which was a broom cupboard and proceeded to attempt to push his room key into the cupboard keyhole! I opened his room door and he was asleep before he hit the bed.

One nice fella is Tommy Grainey.

JIMMY HORNBY

Former Wigan and Lancashire wingman, Jimmy Hornby, was at the club at the time a very tough former player was the coach at Central Park. The coach tried to stop a strike threat by the players after a good cup win in the first round away from home saw them get a much easier draw at home in the second round against a second division side. The board offered a smaller bonus in round two than the players had received in round one and a strike threatened. The outcome was a fall-out between players and coach as the players refused to withdraw their threat and the coach, frustrated about the whole matter, offered any two of the 'Wiganers' outside to settle it behind the stand. 'Now select your two men and I'll be outside waiting for the pair of softies, because I've yet to meet two Wiganers that I can't beat together,' the uptight coach offered, and outside he went, slamming the door behind him.

Always the diplomat, Jimmy Hornby said, 'Did he say Wiganers?, Well he can't mean me, I'm from Billinge.'

ANONYMOUS

A chap was given the job as club secretary at one club I worked at but later one of the directors sacked him for fiddling. 'See what's become of all those gold points from the brewery' the director asked me (those that could be exchanged for gifts). I supplied him with a copy of the gifts claimed. 'A leather briefcase, yes, I can accept that, and a gold plated pen and pencil set, yes, that as well as he may have needed them to do the job, but what is this?' the director said as he checked the gifts, 'A Yamaha freestanding organ! What was he going to do with that, give us a half-time recital?'

Hard men these directors!

LEN CASEY

My old mate Len Casey was up before the disciplinary committee, with the former Rochdale Hornets boss, Jack Grindrod, in the chair. Len was a regular visitor to the disciplinary sessions, so much so, that it was mooted they had a plate with his name on it, screwed onto the defendant's chair. The charge was that Len was sent off for a late tackle that left an opponent prostrate on the ground. As Len entered the Council Chamber, Mr Grindrod, asked Len, 'Have you brought your club video Len?' The Hull KR forward said that he had and the acting secretary, Mr Eddy Bottomly, checked to see if the tape was at the correct setting and started the machine.

The incident flashed onto the screen and Len's slightly high tackle knocked not only the opponent out but also the trilby hat off a spectator in the third row of the stand! Sharp breaths were inhaled by the committee as they witnessed this 'accidental' collision of Len's forearm against the poor bloke's nose. 'Give us a minute Len, will you,' and Len retired to the ante-room, or as some called it the pre-execution room. A few minutes later Len was called back in and sat down in the chair. Mr Grindrod put on his 'posh' voice and said, 'We have looked at the tape Len and we think you were very late into the tackle. Have you anything to say before sentence?'

Len, looking like a choirboy said 'I know I was late chairman, but I got there as quickly as I could'.

Four matches the poor lad got!

17

OVERSEAS PLAYERS - BOTH WAYS

RICHARD L SEDDON, LIONEL COOPER AND OTHER HEROES

In late September, 1907 a ship docked at Folkestone, Kent, carrying a precious cargo. It was Gold, pure Gold. To be honest the cargo was called, the 'All Golds', a group of young athletes from down under, led by a manager called, A H Baskerville. It was the first tour of this country by a predominately New Zealand 13 aside Northern Union team, who wore the famous all black strip of that country, complete with the silver fern over the heart.

Baskerville must have been some character, as legend has it that some of the squad had to double up as stokers on the steam-driven liner to pay for part of their ticket across. And the All Gold part of their nickname was given because they were supposed to be paid expenses, but again, the expenses started only when Baskerville had received a cut of the gate money from the clubs they played on tour.

Two very interesting players were amongst the squad and these two men went on to be legends of the game in their own right and both left a legacy that lasts to this day. LB Todd – Lance Todd – was one of the All Golds and later graced the Salford 'Red Devils' team before moving into the administration side of the game whilst also becoming a top journalist. And to this day, the man of the match award, given to the outstanding player of the Challenge Cup Final, the Lance Todd Trophy, named after LB Todd, is decided by a vote amongst the journalists from the various newspapers covering the day.

The second important figure was a man after whom a medal of great significance is still presented annually in Australia to the best and fairest young player in rugby league and has been won in the past by some immortal names down under. Dally Messenger was the player and he became the greatest of his time. The Australians honoured his memory by naming the coveted 'Dally M' medal after him. For a youngster playing the game in Australia to win the Dally M is the greatest achievement possible, apart from a full international 'Green and Gold', or, a State of Origin jersey.

Dally Messenger's defection to the Northern Union 13-a-side game caused tremendous consternation throughout the Southern Hemisphere as he was the leading player in the established 15-a-side game in Australia. It shows Baskerville's silver tongue, to be able to talk a superstar of those times into making the longest trip on the planet on only spits and promises! But get him he did and the rugby league world will be forever grateful to AH Baskerville, for without his eye for a business opening, his cheek in organising his players to be stokers, and his all round streetwise operating, we may well have never had tours and the 13-a-side code in both Australia and New Zealand may not have prospered to the level at which it is today. But a few years earlier than Baskerville's tour, another tour went out to Australia and met with a sad end!

A poignant little story, which in its way helps us to realise what sport was like way back in 1888. In the summer of that year a team of well-to-do young sportsmen undertook a tour of Australia to play the comparatively new game of rugby football. Tours in those far-off days were totally different to today and, if necessary, teams played various types of games simply to participate in sport.

The captain of the tour was a young Manchester man named Richard L Seddon. Richard was recently engaged to be married and prepared for this final sportsmen's tour before settling down to married life and starting up in business in the city. He was of fine athletic build, standing over 6 feet tall and weighing around 15 stone, big for those days he was a forward in the rugby game and a fearsome tackler.

Richard was an all-round sportsman, a cricketer of no mean ability, a strong swimmer and captain of the Manchester Rowing Club. Sailing into Melbourne the tourists were invited to play a combined sportsmen's club at football and received the shock of their young lives when, on arriving at the venue, found not a pitch that resembled either a rugby or football pitch, but an oval. The football challenge was indeed a new game soon to be renamed Aussie Rules Football!

Not dismayed, our intrepid tourists brushed quickly up on the rules of this strange game, but as it involved kicking and catching it suited them well and, after some early hiccups, the Brits went on to beat Melbourne by a handy score.

Sailing around the bottom of the continent, Sydney was the next stop and a couple of wins had the tourists happy and playing with confidence. The third game was against a Combined University side and was played one half at football and the other at rugby with Seddon's men winning both halves.

The tourists then sailed further up the eastern coast to play the strong Newcastle and District Representative team, in what was an unofficial 'Test' match. But the day before, Richard wrote to his fiancée, professing his love and admiration of her and expressing his desire to return and set up a home for them both after their forthcoming marriage. The letter sailed away to England one hour before the tourists raised the anchor for Newcastle, which in those days was a haven for Cornish and Welsh expats, as it was a thriving coal mining community.

Because of its links with the rugby playing South West of the British Isles, the Newcastle District team were a very competitive side and Richard L Seddon's men just managed a win but only by a few points.

After the game a group of rugby enthusiasts invited the squad to stay in the historic town of Maitland for a few days and while there, visit the famous vineyards at West Maitland. A couple of days relaxing and visiting friends of the enthusiasts soon had the sports-loving Seddon eager to get involved with something other than eating and tasting the wines, so when the day came for the team to visit the vineyards, Richard, having been told about the famous rapids and riptides in the beautiful Hunter River, fancied taking on the wide river as, after all, he was the captain of the Manchester Rowing Club! So the team went west to taste the grape and Richard and a couple of rowing lovers went to take on the Hunter River.

Richard L Seddon was caught in the riptide in his single skiff and overturned. He was last seen alive swimming powerfully towards the far bank of the river but was caught up again by another surge of the tide and was lost, drowned.

His body was recovered some days later and with the young man being so far from home it was decided to bury him near to the river that claimed his life. His team mates were held to make the decision whether or not to bury him at sea but agreed on the land burial when the good people of Maitland, completely overcome by the grief of the tragedy, subscribed a fee to pay for a plot in Maitland cemetery and provide a magnificent headstone.

Richard L Seddon had lost his parents as a young man and had very few relatives who could undertake the difficulties of such a dreadful journey to bring his remains home. His fiancée never married, and the young captain of that disastrous tour is at rest 13,000 miles from Manchester.

To this day a family in Maitland looks after his grave and that family have done so generation after generation, since the day he died and now and again, as a pilgrimage, rugby union tourists sometimes call in to say 'Hi' to Richard L Seddon, captain of the 1888 tour.

But it was the players, mostly from Australia and New Zealand, who provided terrific entertainment for the huge crowds that flocked to see the strength, pace and skills of those magic men from far off places. South Africa also had an impact through some excellent players, mostly three-quarters, but it was the Aussies and the Kiwis that impressed most when ours was a fledgling game, seeking to fill a hunger of release for thousands of northern working class people who could watch their heroes and escape the drudgery, hard work, or even the oppressing unemployment, for 80 minutes on a Saturday afternoon.

My home town club, Leeds, brought their first ever overseas player from the far reaches of New Zealand when in the 1908–09 season the club captured an exciting wing three-quarter, JA Lavery, who although playing in only a handful of games, scored four tries. Little did he know that he was the first of many – too many, some people these days say. But suddenly in the season 1910–11 a name began to appear regularly on the try scoring charts, Albert Rosenfeld of Huddersfield, when in that season he was joint top try scorer along with his team mate, Kitchen and J Miller of Wigan, all with 40 tries each. This prolific Australian wingman went on to head the try scoring table for the next four seasons: in 1911–12 he scored 78 tries, 56 in 1912–13, in 1913–14 he scored 80 a record number in a season to this day, and in 1914–15 he registered 56 tries.

The team, Huddersfield, in which Rosenfeld played wearing the superb claret and gold jerseys, were dubbed 'The Team of All Talents' when in one season, 1914–15, they completed the unbelievable task of winning all four cups, The Challenge Cup, the Yorkshire Cup, the Championship title and the Yorkshire League title, a feat only achieved three times in the games history, Hunslet in 1907–08, Huddersfield and Swinton in 1927–28, the latter, of course, winning the Lancashire Cup and Lancashire League. And the power of the Huddersfield three-quarters of those days is evident when we find that Rosenfeld's regular centre partner, Tommy Gleeson, ran in 45 tries in the same season that his wingman had the record 80! Add to this the presence of Fartown's other centre, the fabulous player known as 'The Prince of Centres' Harold Wagstaff and one can appreciate the wealth of brilliant talent that was on show at Huddersfield back then.

Rosenfeld's prodigious scoring run looks even more awesome when the statistics are studied. His 80 tries were scored in 42 games. The 50 try mark was reached in 25 games and his old record of 78 tries was equalled with a hat-trick against Keighley and broken against Hull Kingston Rovers three days later, on 28th March. He had seven tries in one match, in the 119 points to 2 demolition of Swinton Park amateurs in the Challenge Cup and registered eleven hat-tricks, scored four tries in a match twice and five tries in a match twice. Only on two occasions has any player come within calling distance of Rosenfeld's fantastic record when in 1951–52, Lionel Cooper also of Huddersfield scored a gallant 71 tries and in 1952–53 Brian Bevan of Warrington registered 72, close, but the record of the player from Sydney's Eastern Suburbs still stands!

Just for the record both Cooper and Bevan, of course, were both Australians. Must be something in their water!

There have been many more overseas players that have graced our game who are worthy of mention but unfortunately most will have to be recorded elsewhere, otherwise we will have another *War and Peace* on our hands and I'll have to change my name to Tolstoy. But of the good early imports, Charley Seeling, a back rower from New Zealand joined Wigan and Dinny Campbell arrived from Australia at Leeds to stay and indeed star at Headingley for many seasons.

Wigan again went into the overseas market but this time to South Africa to sign two big men, Van Roohan and Van Heardon. Dinny Campbell went home to Australia but still served the Leeds club by recommending two excellent backs, Frank O'Rourke, a centre of tremendous strength and pace and a young Queensland stand-off who would become a legend at Headingley, Jeff Moores. Moores in turn brought over a couple of years later a tall, lean wingman from the small town of Toowoomba. Eric Harris was his name and still today, as Tom Van Vollenhoven is at St Helens, he is revered almost as a saint!

Eric Harris played 383 games for the Loiners between 1930–31 and 1939–40 and scored 391 tries. His nickname of 'The Toowoomba Ghost' was given by the Swinton full-back, Scott, when in the 1932 Challenge Cup Final at Wigan, he covered Harris's break down the touchline, only to inexplicably miss him and Harris went over for the cup winning try. After the match the press asked the usually sound tackler, Scott, how he had fluffed the tackle, 'I honestly don't know. He was there in my sights and I don't miss those touchline tackles as they have nowhere to go, but he just disappeared, like a ghost'. The name was born and how Eric Harris had disappeared was that he had used his trade-mark evasive quality, the change of pace. He was there, then zoom, he had gone. Scott could just not understand how he could have missed him, but Harris was a master of that trick.

The middle 1930s saw some good overseas internationals arrive here, Markham, the powerful Australian runner came to Huddersfield, Fred French the Kiwi full-back came to Barrow, Cecil Fifield the strong Aussie Test centre arrived at the Boulevard, Hull and the Aussie Test centre sensation Dave Brown, the prematurely bald points machine joined Warrington.

In 1933, the Wigan Highfield club moved lock, stock and barrel to play as London Highfield at the White City Stadium in the country's capital. They folded shortly afterward but the need for a professional rugby league club in London was there to be seen. Two clubs were formed, Acton and Willesden, and then Streatham and Mitcham. The big Maori All Black centre Charley Smith joined Streatham and Mitcham and not long after, Smith's cousin, the great Maori All Black and ace goal kicker, George Nepia joined him at the London club. Both clubs lasted only a short time and Nepia and Smith headed up north to be signed by the Halifax club.

Again, immediately after the end of the Second World War, movements began with top Aussie and Kiwi players signing up to come over and play in the Rugby Football League. Harry Bath the terrific Australian forward joined Barrow but later moved down to Warrington to gain a massive reputation with his power play.

Folklore in Leeds tells of a winter's training evening when a slender, balding Australian merchant seaman arrived asking for a trial game with a letter of recommendation from his former team in Australia. As he stripped to don his training gear, the management in the dressing room had a little laugh together when, seeing his frail build and spindle legs, they asked each other, 'Is this bloke joking? He's too old and too weak to play our game!' So, the Leeds club thanked him for his time in coming to Headingley from his port of release, Liverpool, and respectfully suggested that he tried his luck at a lesser club. He did, he went to Warrington and played his first game for them on 17th November 1945. On 23rd April 1962 he played his final game for the 'Wire' having notched up 740 tries for them. His total tries, including those in Representative, Other Nationalities and two seasons at Blackpool Borough, is still a record in a career, 796 in total. Oh yes, his name is Brian Bevan!

'Bev' played his final game in professional rugby league on 22nd February 1964. Ask any Wigan supporter who was at this particular game, 'Which was the best of the 796 tries that Bev scored' and they will say, the one at Central Park when he collected the ball inches from his own line, right on the corner flag and after beating man, after man, scored in the diagonal corner, a run of around 120 yards allowing for the cross field run and the side-steps he put in. The local newspaper in Wigan printed a plan of the run on the back page, showing the Wigan defenders he beat on the way, and reckoned that he beat the full thirteen team members in the run. In today's disciplined defensive performances it's hard to say if Bev could have gone all that way untackled but Wigan, in those days were renowned for their solid defence, and anyway it's nice to think that he would have done it, as to score 796 tries, he must have had something!

A final word on the great Aussie, Brian Bevan. Some years after his retirement, and by that time he must have been very near his sixties, a letter appeared in my local newspaper showing a cutting from a weekly Torquay advertising paper. It told of the extraordinary deeds of an elderly gentleman playing for the Torquay Rugby Union Club's fifth team on the wing, and this elderly chap has just broken the all-time Torquay club try scoring record for the season, with, I believe, a total of over 50 tries. The old chap was named as Mr B Bevan! Now I don't know if Mr B Bevan was the great man, but I did hear that he had retired down there to that beautiful part of England. But then again Bev may well have just gone for a fortnight holiday, guested for Torquay and scored the tries in two matches! He was brilliant, and as a young man in the late 1950s, I had the privilege of playing against him. Again I say, privilege.

Huddersfield stirred too when, immediately after the 1946 tour, they announced the signing of three of the most entertaining Australian players ever to grace our game. Full-back Johnny Hunter, he of the defence splitting runs and fearless tackling, Lionel Cooper, an Aussie Test wingman and scorer of two tries against the touring Lions in the 1946 series, who at 6 foot and 15 stone and with speed, was a formidable opponent indeed and the third was the exquisite footballer, Pat Devery, who was equally at home at stand-off or centre. Cooper and Devery had represented Australia in all three Tests in the 1946 series with Devery operating at stand-off each game.

Hunter's natural game was one of fast counter attack, and pity the poor kicker who placed his punt in the wrong area as Hunter would run the ball back at them with interest and his linking in from the set scrum, as he sliced between the centres, was a joy to behold.

Pat Devery was a subtle player with fine little touches to his game, classical when running with the ball, his superb ability to create openings for his wing partner were features of this wonderful footballers make up. Devery's defensive qualities too were of the highest standard and his copybook tackling around the legs could have been shown on any coaching film of 'how to tackle correctly'.

Lionel Cooper was the type of player hardly ever seen before in this country. Because of his powerful build, teams were known to play forwards on the wing to oppose him, size for size. A solid block of a player, Cooper had pace that belied his bulk and possessed a steam-hammer hand off that created many tries for him. His favourite ploy though was to use his hips as a 'fend'. As a tackler aimed at his waist in the tackle, as it was impossible to bring him to ground around the thighs as they were immensely strong, Cooper would bump off the tackler by hitting him with his hip, so strong on the run was he.

As a youngster I saw these three Aussies many times, both at Fartown – what memories that evokes – and Headingley and the battles between the pace of the Leeds flying Scottish wingman, Andrew Turnbull, against the power of Cooper were worth the entrance fee alone. I recall in a tight match at Headingley, Devery putting in a perfect kick for Cooper to chase and with Turnbull covering the kick it developed into an all out race between these two fine players. It was almost a certainty that the 'Flying Scotsman', Turnbull, would have won the straight race, but the vastly experienced Cooper hit Turnbull with a perfectly fair shoulder charge, sending the Leeds man sprawling to the calls of 'foul' by the Leeds fans. Cooper retrieved the ball and planted it down for a fair try.

I remember vividly dashing home to read my *rules of the game*, little blue book, and found it there in black and white that it is allowed to shoulder charge if two players are chasing the ball, side by side, as Cooper and Turnbull were. So Lionel Cooper taught me one of the rules of the game that I didn't know! He also picked up a Challenge Cup winners medal in 1953 in Huddersfield's 15-10 win over St Helens at Wembley.

Coopers reign as the premier wingman of his era was

always challenged by Brian Bevan and in the ten seasons between 1945–46 and 1954–55 Bevan topped the try count on five occasions and Cooper three. The big Aussie was top in 1948–49 with 60 tries, in 1951–52 with 71 tries and in 1954–55 with 66.

I was transferred from Hull FC to Dewsbury in 1957 and the coach that signed me at the old Crown Flatt was Lionel Cooper. He had a bee in his bonnet about the Dewsbury forwards defence on the previous weekend as I trained for the first time with my new club. One tough kid in particular took offence at the coach's remarks and insisted that he could tackle, in fact insisted to the point of virtually challenging the coach to run at him and he would prove that he could tackle. That was his first mistake. His second mistake was to go high for the great Lionel Cooper as the coach trundled down the Crown Flatt slope under the floodlights on the grandstand and the steam-hammer came out of mothballs to flatten the cocky forward. The kid's third mistake was to demand another shot at the big Aussie, who only two seasons before had scored 66 tries against first class company. Lionel obliged and this time our misguided forward aimed, like so many before, at the bulky waist line. This time the hip caught the brave, but sadly mismatched player, and that was the end of his training session. He should have known that the legend Cooper had a bit left. Too much for him!

Huddersfield also gained the services of the former New Zealand sprint champion and All Black wingman Peter Henderson. This extremely fast finisher also represented New Zealand in the Olympic Games and reached the 100 metre final. Quick indeed.

Halifax gained a cracking Kiwi centre in the shape of Tommy Lynch and grand little Bramley scooped up an Australian centre, who unfortunately for the Villagers, was too good a player for them to keep. Big brother Leeds moved in and in a deal beneficial to both clubs this grand player, Bob Bartlett, moved up Kirkstall Hill to the marble halls of Headingley.

The two clubs with a strong tradition of bringing over Antipodeans, Wigan and Leeds, had also had their scouts working overtime and a tremendous capture for the Central Park brigade in 1946 was, in the opinion of many, the best Kiwi ever to play over here, Ces Mountford. One of the greatest accolades given to Ces was that even over the 'hill' in Yorkshire, kids playing touch and pass all wanted to be Ces Mountford! He was unbelievable. Quick, intelligent, brave and with the double ability to make play for his centres and be a match winning try scorer to boot! Fellow Kiwi, Brian Nordgren, the free scoring speedy wingman joined the legend Mountford and his best scoring season was 1949–50 when he registered 57 tries.

Leeds' major signing in 1946 was the New Zealand Rugby Union international full-back, HE (Bert) Cook, the man who possessed two odd sized feet, the right foot took a size four and the left a size three, small feet but a prodigious goal kicker. One in particular that will forever be remembered was in the Challenge Cup third round at Wigan in 1947, when with Leeds in front by three points to nil thanks to a Gareth Price try, were awarded a penalty kick two yards inside their own half and angled to the posts in ankle deep mud. Up stepped Bert Cook, built a mound of mud, placed the heavy old leather ball on top and brought the biggest cheer for years from a big Leeds following as the ball sailed over the crossbar and between the posts from his wonder kick. A likeable always smiling man, Bert Cook moved to Keighley as player/coach, then came to Dewsbury to take over from Lionel Cooper. Again I was lucky enough to play both with Bert and under his coaching regime and for someone who saw his first game for Leeds against York at

Headingley as a ten year old kid, it was a tremendous thrill for me.

The next signing in January 1947 was one that had the biggest influence on me in a lifetime of watching rugby league. Leeds signed the best second row forward that I ever saw, Arthur Clues. I have described big Arthur earlier but saved this little tale until now. Arthur had moved from Leeds to arch rivals Hunslet and I was playing at loose forward in a league match at Crown Flatt against my childhood hero. I was lucky enough to have made two good breaks and almost set up two tries early in the game when, slap, a smack across my face nearly loosened all my teeth. It came from my hero who, grabbing me by the collar, pulled me to him and said, 'We don't want any f****** more of those today, young 'un,' and I did as I was told. He is still my hero, slap or no slap. At least I got some reaction from the one and only big Arthur Clues.

I saw his first game for Leeds. It was in a defeat by Hull FC at Headingley but the late, wonderful, big Arthur made that dull winters day seem like summer time!

Another huge smiling man was signed from South African Rugby Union in the form of the giant, Jack Pansegrouw but he was transferred to Halifax after a short stay at Leeds and the strong Maori centre Ike Proctor came the other way from Thrum Hall. Trevor Allen the Australian Rugby Union centre joined Leigh and Workington Town secured the classical Tony Paskins to form a superb centre partnership with Eppie Gibson. An exciting stand-off was also brought over from Australia when 'Fizzer' Dawson went to Workington. He was followed by the tough, durable Aussie, John Mudge. Wakefield Trinity signed Dennis Booker from down under. And the tall, robust Australian forward Rex Mossop, who later became a respected journalist and TV game caller back home, joined Leigh. Leeds bought two thirds of the Australian Rugby Union front row by signing prop 'Wallaby' Bob McMaster and hard case hooker Ken Kearney and earlier had signed the utility back and excellent servant of the club, Ted Verrencamp and the side stepping wonder winger, Len Kenny, who only lasted a short time before moving to Leigh.

Bradford Northern introduced the fine pair of Kiwis, Big Jack McLean the powerful wingman who had 63 tries in 1951–52, 59 in 1952–53, 52 in 1953–54 and 61 in 1955–56 and that superb full-back Joe Phillips. Leeds went to Hull to sign the strong Bruce Ryan, who was not only a cracking wingman but also doubled as a night club singer! Another South African, centre Alan Skene joined Wakefield Trinity to form himself as the rapier and the stupendous Neil Fox as the broadsword. Trinity also signed Colin Greenwood, a utility back from the Union of South Africa. Not to be outdone, Dewsbury imported three Maori players, full-back Johnny Wilson, centre 'George' Nepia (not THE George Nepia) and 'Smut' Smith a tough nut prop. Nepia went home, Smith moved into Lancashire but Johnny Wilson stayed in the West Riding, had many seasons playing for Bramley and became a well known landlord in several Leeds pubs until his passing.

Saints went into the South African market to buy an absolute belting wingman, the 'Van', Tom Van Vollenhoven. A prince of wingmen Vollenhoven topped the try charts for three years running when from 1958–59 through to 1960–61 he registered 62, 54 and 59 tries. Saints also brought over South African's, Len Kileen, who headed the try chart in 1965–66 with 32, and Jan Prinsloo.

The superb Aussie, Arthur Beetson arrived for a spell with Hull Kingston Rovers and was an outstanding capture. Beetson was a tough Queenslander who had suddenly appeared on the Aussie scene and he made a huge impact on the game over there, starting against our successful 1970 tourists, with his skilful ball distribution and ability to stand in the tackle and deliver defence splitting passes. He was also a hard man as a little tale from a very respected prop forward testifies. Dave Horn played for many, many seasons at Bramley and any prop who tangled with him will tell you that he was one big, tough unit. In a mid-week evening game at the old Craven Park ground, big Artie Beetson and the equally big Dave Horn had been at it hammer and tongs all night. At the hooter to end the game, players were shaking hands, as players do, when Beetson saw Dave Horn walking towards him. Now big Dave reckons that he was going to shake hands, but, and he told me this some years later, big Artie thought Dave was coming to carry on their disagreements of the past 80 minutes and as Dave offered his hand, Artie threw his Sunday punch and said, 'Goodnight' to Dave.

'First time in my life I was knocked out, and I fell for the oldest trick in the book,' said wistful Dave Horn many years later. But Artie must have carried some fire-power to knock out the ultra tough Dave Horn!

Halifax acquired the services of Chris Anderson as player/coach and did wonderfully well under his guidance. Chris went on to bigger things and had a spell as coach at his former club Canterbury Bankstown, then coached the excellent Melbourne Storm to a Premiership win before becoming a successful Australian National team coach. His success at Thrum Hall, which included the exciting win at Wembley over St Helens in 1987 by 19 points to 18 (who can forget John Pendlebury's last second tackle over his own try line that caused Kiwi Mark Elia to drop the ball, and win the cup for Halifax), was based on the signing of several good young Australians and two 'old heads', himself and Graham Eadie, the former Australian international full-back, and a touring mate of Anderson's in 1978. He signed up players who would later play international football for Australia in

Martin Bella and Paul Langmark, and others such as Keith Neller and Michael Hagen who had good careers in Sydney football.

Hull FC enticed a foursome of terrific Kiwis over in Fred Ah Kuoi, James Leuluai, Dane O'Hara and Gary Kemble and brought the king-pin of scrum halves from Paramatta, Peter Stirling, who inspired not only the 'Parra' club and Hull FC but Australia too for many years. Peter's international mate and the worlds best utility player, Brett Kenny, joined Wigan along with a tremendous aboriginal wingman, the great John Ferguson. Later Test prop Greg Dowling and the brilliant 'Zip-Zip'man, Steve Ella, another Test star, went to Central Park. Howie Tamati the Kiwi hooker had a spell at Wigan but the signing that grabbed the imagination of all rugby lovers was the arrival at Wigan of the man himself, 'Inga the Winger', All Black legend, Va'aiga Tuigamala, who with Frano Botica and Sam Panapa plus, a little earlier, Graeme West, formed a strong backbone to the side. Saints signed the mighty Mal Meninga and the big Aussie Test man played a huge part in Saints winning the 1984–85 Premiership trophy. Wakefield Trinity did their bit too by bringing over the fabulous Wally Lewis to play for a few months and Hull Kingston Rovers had a goodly share of Kiwis in the internationals, Mark Broardhurst, Gary Prohm and Gordon Smith

Warrington introduced John Wright, a big Aussie forward, in the 1970s then gained a tremendous trio of forwards from down under in Kiwi Test player, Kevin Tamati, a hard working utility packman in Bob Jackson and another Aussie, Les Boyd, a fearsome front rower who had both Test caps and State of Origin experience. Leigh had two good Kiwis too in the form of Shane Varley, a Test scrum-half, and Jeff Clarke who also represented his country.

As we come in to the Super League era, lots of overseas players were still recruited but somehow they were not all of the calibre of Mal Meninga, Wally Lewis, Brett Kenny or Peter Stirling. There was no one of the calibre of Kevin Tamati, Greg Dowling, Harry Bath or Arthur Clues, just a load of players, apart from a handful, that had not played at the highest level down under but served their purpose as workman like players without being a Lionel Cooper, Brian Bevan, Jack McLean or Tom Van Vollenhoven. We know there are not many of those in a pound and that the influx of money in the Aussie game has meant that, with respect, the bigger contracts are not available in Sydney if you are approaching the 30 years mark and that is the type of player who will openly admit that when their days are through in Sydney footy they will have a few seasons in England, because our level is that much lower than over there! Whether or not that helps our game I would not know, possibly it doesn't, but the men in the boardrooms have changed too in these so-called enlightened days and there are few Bill Boardalls and Harry Jepsons, much to our loss.

Not all the traffic has been one way, although it was until top players such as Dave Bolton moved from Wigan to Australia and Lewis Jones headed out from Leeds to become an early settler to a club called Wentworthville. In quick succession our game lost the services of Mal Reilly (Castleford), and Cliff Watson and Tommy Bishop (both of St Helens). Other early leavers were Yorkshire county centre, Bryan Todd (Halifax, Bradford Northern and Saints), Dick Huddart (Saints), Ken Noble (Huddersfield) and Charlie Renilson (Halifax). Two of our top performers went to the same club when Mick (Stevo of Sky TV) Stephenson of Dewsbury and Wigan's Bill Ashhurst were snapped up by the Penrith Panthers. Stevo had just starred in our World Cup win of 1972 and was on the brink of many Great Britain caps when he and the terrific Bill Ashurst, also a young international with his top flight career in front of him, decided that

Australia was for them.

The big, speedy second rower from Hull KR, Phil Lowe had a good run with the Manly club. John Gray (Wigan) a recent convert from Rugby Union, went back to Australia almost immediately after the 1974 tour, and stayed there. Castleford's Gary Stephens and Steve Norton had successful spells in Australia and the powerful front rower whose career took in Castleford and St Helens over here, Kevin Ward, went across to Manly and knocked 'em dead with his strong running and hard defence. The next two players to join the full-time exodus and stay long term were both Wigan players, Andy Platt and Denis Betts. But just before this, a breed of young ambitious players, obviously chasing the money, were attempting a dangerous career with the advent of the back-to-back seasons, playing one in Australia then the next in England, then back to Australia and so on. I would guess that possibly as a three-quarter, Gary Schofield (Hull FC) played the most back to backs with Lee Crooks (also Hull FC) may be the one with the most as a forward. Des Drummond (Leigh) and Joe Lydon (Wigan) did a couple and the great Ellery Hanley had spells at Balmain and Western Suburbs.

Mike Gregory of Warrington went over to Australia for a season as did Brian Noble of Bradford Northern and the Wigan pair of Shaun Edwards and Andy Gregory. Adrian Morley (ex Leeds) and Keith Mason (Saints) are two of the latest players, both forwards, who have benefited from a spell in Australian football. Indeed Morley is arguably the best forward playing according to some good judges.

So there you are, some are missing in this list of players who have starred on the other side of the world, and as I have said not all are mentioned because of space. But when you look at the quality of the early leavers from the British game one can see why we dipped a bit in international football.

18

THE JOINING OF THE HANDLING CODES

UNION PLAYERS WITH FALSE NAMES!

Money was the biggest reason for the breakaway in 1895 when the northern clubs parted company with the Rugby Football Union. It is well recorded that broken time payment from work caused the rift that forced the north from the south. Saturday's working shift ended no earlier than 2:00pm in the days prior to the split giving the working man little chance to enjoy either playing or watching his chosen sport of rugby football. The well-to-do gentlemen and their sons had no problem with this and gradually, as various factory acts lessening the working times came in, it made it a little easier for the working class to participate in the playing side of things, but they still had to stand time off work and the lost revenue should an away game result in 'breaking time'.

In no way would the governors of the Union allow broken time payments as they considered it the first step towards professionalism. The defection from the RFU by the Northern clubs devastated the Union game. Before the split the north country players were the key men in regular victories over Wales, Scotland and Ireland and the counties of the north, particularly Yorkshire and Lancashire, regularly provided the 'best' players, with a tougher, harder home background than their southern counterparts.

In the one hundred and odd years since, the RFU never forgave, and still don't seem to forgive and the tales of pure hatred of the northern game are told by many players, particularly from Wales, who committed the worst heresy: that of 'Going North'. The Union clubs, who stayed true to the 15-a-side code here in the North, somehow became stauncher in their hatred of 'the other code' than their Southern brothers. These clubs were usually situated in the wealthier rural areas, on the outskirts of the larger towns and in the villages and hamlets still governed by the mill owner and his family, who most likely employed everyone in that village or hamlet, and even dictated how they used their leisure time away from the mill!

So it was until even only a few short months ago when I had a call to speak at a charity dinner at a traditional small, but well-known, rugby union club. There behind the bar I saw an ancient oil painting of a union game played on this club's ground in the middle 1890s between Yorkshire and Lancashire. On closer inspection one could clearly see the features, all different, of the various players, and about four of the eighteen or so players depicted had had their faces obliterated, just their faces, so as not to spoil the whole painting, The barman, an old retainer by the club, didn't know me from Adam and when I asked him about the rubbed out faces he said with venom, 'Oh, those. The rats turned professional with Manningham in 1895.'

David Watkins the superb dual international and idol of Welsh rugby union until he signed for Salford, tells of not being allowed in the Cardiff clubhouse for a drink with his family who still lived in Wales. Refused entry because he played rugby league, and the irony was that the clubhouse was built with the aid of a sports council grant, which says, *sport for all, with no bar on colour, creed or religion!* (Except rugby league?) At another time around 1984 when

I was coaching Leeds, I was allowed entry into the Morley Rugby Union Club and made welcome as a fully paid-up member. The coach at Morley at the time was a well-respected Yorkshire County forward, and as they had a crucial Yorkshire Cup semi-final against Wakefield RU in the offing, he asked me if I would go to a training session to introduce a couple of set piece moves near the opponents try line to use in the semi-final. I agreed, but suddenly the coach remembered that there was a Yorkshire County Committee meeting at the club that training night. 'If they see you coaching us they will kick us out of the Cup,' he said. So the training session was moved from the main pitch, down to the third team's pitch, which was some distance away from the clubhouse in which the County meeting was being held. 'One other thing,' the coach asked me, 'can you come the back way in, through Bruntcliffe Cemetery so no-one sees you?' Imagine me as the Leeds Rugby League coach, in the middle of winter, in the pitch black, picking my way through the cemetery with a couple of new graves open, to coach a rugby union team in a semi-final, just to outsmart the Yorkshire County Committee, and with the Morley coach the instigator! Brigadier General McGregor Kendall-Carpenter would turn in his grave if he had known, the bounder, by gad!

I did cheat much earlier though when I was a young player having a spot of financial argument with my first professional club, Hull FC. I was in dispute and staying away in protest when my best mate, who had joined a local junior union club, asked me if I wanted a game as Hull FC would not give me a permit to play amateur rugby league. I said, 'Yes please,' and went, cautiously, to training expecting to find lawyers, bankers and doctors in the dressing room. Instead the room was full of rugby league lads all playing under false names, and I have never seen so many frightened faces as there were on the Saturday of the match, the whole side was petrified that we would be found out. But the host club, in those far off days, had never seen such open rugby as no one would kick the ball. All we did was run it no matter where we were on the field!

I played about six times and although playing at loose forward and second row in my own game, was asked to play fly-half. I reckoned I was Cliff Morgan running around, but only in my dreams. Now there was a good player and a gentleman!

On the reverse side of that, we once played against Leeds A at Headingley for Dewsbury A and had a trialist union forward playing for us. We wore white shorts and the trialist used his own shorts, white, with pockets! Behind at half-time, and in those days you stayed on the field and did not retire into the dressing room, my favourite coach of all time, Bill Smith, was explaining how we could win this one, with his team listening intently to him. Suddenly in the breeze, there on the Headingley pitch, a Spangle wrapper blew slowly past Bill (for those that don't remember, Spangles were a popular fruit sweet of the time) then another blew past our coach, and a third. Bill looked around him and saw the trialist putting a packet of Spangles back into his shorts pocket. 'Give them here,' Bill advised and the reserves told us that Bill passed the Spangles around during the second half and between them they ate the lot.

'These rugby union men coming into our game and eating Spangles, whatever next?' Bill said to us, with a smile on his face. But that's what he always advised, 'Enjoy this lovely game, and play with a smile on your face'.

I hope you have had a smile thinking of the players of years gone by and how our beautiful game was.